D1052803

At the Helm

At the Helm

Business Lessons for

Navigating Rough Waters

Peter Isler
and Peter Economy

CURRENCY

DOUBLEDAY

New York London Toronto Sydney Auckland

A Currency Book
PUBLISHED BY DOUBLEDAY
a division of Random House, Inc.
1540 Broadway, New York, New York 10036

CURRENCY and DOUBLEDAY are
trademarks of Doubleday, a division
of Random House, Inc.

Thanks to J-Class Management, Inc., for granting
permission to use excerpts from its website
(www.jclass.com). Reprinted by permission of
J-Class Management, Inc.

Book design by Dana Leigh Treglia

Library of Congress Cataloging-in-Publication Data

Isler, Peter, 1955–
At the helm: business lessons for navigating rough waters /
Peter Isler and Peter Economy—1st ed.
     p.   cm.
1. Success in business.   2. Sailing.   I. Economy, Peter.
II. Title.
HF5386.I74   2000
650.1—dc21   99-41178
                                            CIP

ISBN: 0-385-49796-2

1   3   5   7   9   10   8   6   4   2

To my mother,
Betty Economy Gritis. Will the circle
be unbroken.

Acknowledgments

I would first and foremost like to thank all the people who took time away from their busy lives to be interviewed for this book. Many are good friends, business associates, former teammates or respected competitors who have helped me a lot over the years. The invaluable insights and experiences that they have shared with us here are the real core and treasure of this book. I would also like to recognize some key people who have had a major influence on my competitive sailing career, including: Ted Jones, Kendrick Wilson, Tom Whidden, and Dennis Conner. And my good friend Lenny Shabes deserves recognition, as he hired me into my first real job—proving to me that a sailor could indeed even exist in the world of business!

Contents

Foreword

What makes a winner? Winning.

What does it take to win? Athletes, businesspeople, and anyone involved in any competition have asked themselves that question. For athletes, the answer is most often found deep down inside their souls. To succeed, athletes first have to have the great confidence in themselves and to know that there is no barrier that they can't overcome. They have to dream bold dreams and have a strong and compelling vision of success that draws them ever forward—and that dulls the pain of hours, weeks, and years of intense workouts, practices, and competition. And they have to work hard—incredibly hard—to achieve their goals. Only then, through a deep commitment to personal excellence, is a winner forged out of the muscle, brains, and sinew of which we are all built.

Is it surprising that these very same qualities can make the difference between someone who is successful in business and someone who is not? They can. And they do.

Success in business requires self-confidence, the kind

that comes from becoming an expert in one's chosen field and from rising to meet the challenges that our clients, customers, and suppliers present us with every day of the week. It requires people who can dream big dreams and then build committed and energized teams of believers to help them achieve those big dreams. And above all, it requires hard work. Lots and lots of hard work.

Sailboat racing is a very dynamic sport. Few who witnessed the adrenaline rush of watching *Stars & Stripes* take back the America's Cup in 1987—broadcast live on television from Perth, Australia—will forget it. The sheer grit and determination of those sailors was palpable—even 9,000 miles away. In few other places will you find an activity that combines so many important business skills—from teamwork, to leadership, to innovation, to ingenuity, to flexibility, and much more—all in one place. The sport of sailboat racing offers lessons that we can all benefit from, no matter what kind of organization we work in or what our places on the organization chart might be.

As authors Peter Isler and Peter Economy richly show in this book, there is a clear and definable link between success in sailboat racing and success in business. It's no coincidence that some of the biggest names in the sports of sailing—Turner, Ellison, David, Koch, Disney, and others—are also some of the most notable successes in the world of business. By reading about their personal experiences in sailing and in business, you can't help but benefit by learning what has made these men and women successful—both on and off the water.

There is no doubt in my mind that being successful in sports can help you be successful in business, as well. Sports are a *great* teacher. As you read these stories of personal commitment and excellence, you will find application to your own organization and to everyday life.

—Phil Knight
Chairman and CEO, Nike, Inc.
Beaverton, Oregon

At the Helm

Chapter One

At the Helm

There are days on the racecourse when you feel like mother nature is reaching deep and throwing her best stuff at you. That was the case during the fifth race of the Challenger Finals for the 1987 America's Cup. As part of Dennis Conner's *Stars & Stripes* team, we had prepared for this day for years, training aboard a series of sixty-five-foot aluminum-hulled sloops in the blustery northeast trade winds off Oahu's south coast, testing ourselves and our boats in conditions that most sailors would consider extremely dangerous. I was on the boat as the navigator, along with tactician Tom Whidden. Dennis was on the helm, and we had a crew of eight other sailors. Another day of twenty-four to twenty-eight-knot winds shouldn't have seemed so tough, but for some reason it did that particular day.

Maybe it had something to do with the competition. Chris Dickson's team aboard the New Zealand challenger, *Kiwi Magic*, had been dominant throughout the three months of trials, losing only once and racking up thirty-seven wins. But the slate had been wiped clean, and we were well into the best-of-seven series. The first team to win four races would earn a shot at the defending Aussies in the America's Cup Match. The losing team would go home—tens of millions of dollars poorer—without so much as a wooden plaque to remember the race by. In the America's Cup, there is no second place.

As the twenty-five-ton sloop pounded upwind in the choppy three- to five-foot waves off Fremantle, Australia, viewers from around the world were tuned in—watching the spectacle live on television. The boat looked part submarine, part sailboat as it sliced through the seas. *Stars & Stripes* had opened up a ten-boat-length lead over the Kiwis when all of a sudden . . . *Bang!* The headsail, made out of ultrastrong Kevlar fibers, exploded—torn to shreds by the combined force of wind and waves. Where once there had been a smooth, wing-shape foil helping to drive the sloop forward, now there were only tatters waving dangerously from the rigging like some long-forgotten flag.

Even from the comfort of a living room several thousand miles away, the next few moments were dramatic—certainly the most memorable moments of the 1987 America's Cup campaign. It was an all-hands-on-deck emergency as eight of the eleven crew members raced up to the foredeck to help pull in the remnants of the sail and quickly get them out of the way. On the pitching foredeck, the old expression, "one hand for yourself and one hand for the ship" took on new meaning.

Unlike a standard ocean-racing sailboat, a 12 Meter has no guardrails—just keeping your balance up there is a very real and ongoing challenge If you're careless or lose your concentration for just a moment, there's *nothing* to keep you from washing into the Indian Ocean. Add to that the task of wrestling a savage wind to get a sail under control and stuffed down below—all the while holding on for dear life—and it's downright insane!

A sailboat can be an incredibly inhospitable place to be. When the seas are churning, and the wind is howling, keeping "one hand for yourself and one hand for the ship" can literally mean the difference between life and death. While few of us are faced with such extreme conditions at work, we are often faced with situations that can make the difference between getting the promotion or recognition we've been long striving for and deserve, or not. Just as on a sailboat, you should keep one hand for yourself—learning new skills, taking on new responsibilities, and promoting your own interests—and one hand for the organization. By focusing your efforts on both fronts, you ensure that your organization, your coworkers and clients will receive maximum benefit from your efforts—and you will optimize your personal performance.

Somehow, we managed to get the one-thousand-plus square feet of bulletproof sailcloth stuffed through the hatch and out of the way down below. If you have ever felt the "fabric" of a modern racing sail, you know that it has a texture much closer to a sheet of light aluminum than to a sheet of cotton. To gather the sail you must somehow get a grasp on this slippery surface, drag it in a few feet, and then reach up and do it again. And all the while you are using every ounce of your strength to pull the sail against the wind—somehow staying glued to a tiny, wet, and slippery foothold. A few feet away from you, a teammate is doing the same thing, and inch by inch you make progress.

As we dragged in the blown-out sail, our boat slowed from 8.5 knots to less than half of its racing speed. *Kiwi Magic* was closing fast as we stuffed the last remnants of the old sail below, and Scotty Vogel prepared a new sail for hoisting. During this time, the bow of the boat was plunging up and down—going through more than ten feet of vertical motion. A split-second of inattention to the boat, or just a bit of bad luck, and one or more of us could have been launched off the bow and into the choppy seas, endangering the other crew members and putting the last nail in the coffin of this particular race.

Fortunately for us, the story had a happy ending. We were able to hoist the new sail before Dickson and his crew could get past us. As the new sail filled and we started picking up speed, you could almost hear the cheers and applause from the millions of TV viewers around the world who had just been treated to one of the most exciting moments in America's Cup history—live! We went on to win the series four races to one and move on to the America's Cup where we found the Aussies were less competitive than the Kiwis. We won the Cup in four straight races and headed home with our trophy to a reception at the White House and a ticker-tape parade down Fifth Avenue.

That moment was certainly a major milestone in our campaign, but the real story started about a week before that when, in training, we had a similar all-hands-on-deck emergency during a practice race with the British team. The conditions at that time were far milder (it was only blowing eighteen knots that day!), but the same group of guys completely whiffed on the recovery. We got the old sail so tangled up on the foredeck that there was no hope of hoisting a new one. Dennis finally headed off the course in disgust over his so-called "professional" crew's inability to solve the problem.

That night, during the tow in back to the dock, the eight guys who had had the "good fortune" to be assigned foredeck duties during emergencies had a meeting to analyze what went wrong. We had gotten the tattered old sail down okay, but then were working so furiously that half the sail got stuffed down the hatch on the left side of the deck and the other half got stuffed down the opening on the right side. It was sailcloth macramé up there on the foredeck—a real mess.

We decided that the problem was not a people problem, but one of organization. What we needed was one voice to focus the best efforts of the crew. Although any emergency might offer several potential courses of action, we needed to settle on just one, so we agreed that bowman Scotty Vogel would be the leader of the gang. In an emergency, he would devise a solution and then inform the crew of the plan. While there was always a chance that someone else might come up with a better plan, we decided that it would be far better to stay focused and move swiftly rather than debate the merits of a particular plan while the competition sailed away.

So, when the jib blew out during the race, we had been there before, and we had a plan for reacting. Scotty looked at the shredded sail and immediately decided on the best way to retrieve it. He quickly divided up responsibilities, and told us what we needed to know ("Stuff it down the starboard hatch . . . *Fast!!!*"). It wasn't easy, but as a team we solved the problem and got the job done, winning the race and keeping the Kiwis on the defensive.

That moment, more than any other, remains etched in the memories of Cup fans around the world. Little do they know that had it not been for the accident during training the result would have been a lot different! And little did I imagine at the time how that particular experience would shape the way I think about sailing.

I have long considered sailing to be a metaphor for life, and so do many others who love the sport. We live and breathe the sport, and it colors almost everything we do. As the years have passed since that Cup victory, I have also begun to see how sailing is a compelling metaphor for business, too. The lessons of teamwork, planning, preparation, and perseverance that served us so well off Fremantle are just as applicable in the world of business as they are out on the water. It's no accident that some of the world's most successful businesspeople are also some of the world's most successful sailboat racers.

In this book, coauthor Peter Economy and I pursue this idea to its logical conclusion. We interviewed more than thirty business leaders, visionaries, students, and practitioners, *all* of whom are well versed in the world of sailboat racing. Some of the names you'll recognize, some you won't. And while some are more successful than others—both on and off the water—they all share a common perspective, a perspective born in the wind, nurtured in the spray of salt water, and put to the test in the heat of competition. It's a perspective that has simultaneously enriched their lives and made them incredibly effective businesspeople.

From the importance of making a total commitment, to building true team effort, to changing course quickly, and more, we have organized the lessons into seven fundamental rules of sailboat racing and business. These rules—some of them honed over hundreds, perhaps even thousands of days of sailing—may seem like common sense. The fact is, however, that they are not common practice. But for those who apply them they will make all the difference in the world.

I hope you enjoy this book as much as Peter and I enjoyed writing it. In the end, it's as much a celebration of sailing as it is a book about business. While we have tried to keep the language from getting too salty—because this book *is* meant, after all, for both sailors *and* nonsailors—we hope you will be captivated by some of the great sea stories that we have gathered and the images of what it's like to be out on the water just messing about in boats.

I hope to see you out there soon!

Chapter Two

The Art of Sailboat Racing and Business

Mention sailboat racing and what picture enters your mind? Sleek boats with billowing sails straining against the wind—reaching for every last ounce of speed as they slice through the waves? Storm clouds on the horizon framing a fleet of wind-powered craft heading out to sea? Water-slicked decks perpetually tilted at inhumanly sharp angles; crew members scurrying about in a frantic ballet of purposeful motion? Champagne corks flying as another victorious crew celebrate their success at the end of a hard-fought race?

Sure, those common images of sailboat racing are all very much a part of the sport. If you look closely, however, you'll find that there is something else lurking just below the surface—something just as essential to the success of sailboat racers as a fast boat, an experienced crew, and the deep pockets of sponsors.

It's business.

There's far more to fielding a successful sailing team than simply showing up at the dock on the day of the race. To win the world's most sought-after races—the prestigious America's Cup, the grueling around-the-world Volvo Ocean Race, the often hellish Sydney to Hobart, the coveted Olympic Gold Medal, and others—it takes years of planning, years of training, years of practice, and not a small amount of luck. It takes leaders with an absolute commitment to winning and a long-range vision of success coupled with a well-trained, talented, and hardworking crew reaping the rewards that true teamwork affords. It takes the most current technology available today and loads of money to keep up with the latest advances in state-of-the-art equipment in a sport that drives participants to seek out even the smallest competitive advantage.

And it takes business smarts—*major* business smarts. A typical America's Cup campaign costs $25 million, and some teams have spent much more. An Olympic campaign, even in a small, one-person boat, can easily get into six figures. Other key races require similar commitments of significant funds, and the kind of high-caliber business talent that will get the right things done at the right time by the right people. Without an effective business organization and support structure to back them up, even the most well-funded team with the best boat and the most talented skipper and crew will be left high and dry during the long process of mounting a successful racing campaign.

Perhaps it's no coincidence then that some of the world's most successful sailors are also some of the world's most successful businesspeople. People like CNN founder and Time Warner vice chairman Ted Turner, winner of the America's Cup in 1977 at the helm of the 12 Meter sloop *Courageous*. Or Larry Ellison, chairman and CEO of computer database management systems software giant Oracle—the world's second-largest software company with $7 billion in annual revenues—who not only survived the deadly 1998 Sydney-to-Hobart yacht race aboard his eighty-foot-long maxi-boat *Sayonara* but won it. Or Roy Disney, vice chairman of the Walt Disney Company, whose seventy-two-foot turbo-sled *Pyewacket* set a new course record of seven days, eleven hours, forty-one minutes, and twenty-seven seconds in the 1999 Transpacific Yacht Race, a downwind sleigh ride in the trade winds from Los Angeles to Honolulu.

The fact is that anyone in business—whether you're an owner, a manager, or a line worker—can learn a lot about improving their performance and creating a more efficient and more effective organization by studying the habits and methods of successful sailboat racers.

And here's the good news: You won't have to get wet to learn them.

On the Water

The start of a race is a place where time is simultaneously accelerated—and suspended—for what seems an eternity. It's probably the only part of a sailboat race where chaos reigns supreme and any thought of an organized plan of attack goes quickly out the window. It's not enough that the skipper and crew have to deal with shifting winds, invisible water currents, and the tune of their own boat and sails. They also have to face a fleet full of boats that are as unpredictable as a spring shower on a warm afternoon in April.

All hands know that the start—especially on a shorter course—is an incredibly important part of the race, and that it often plays a huge role in its final outcome. If the sailors have done their research, they'll pretty much know exactly where they need to be at the beginning of the race. In sailboat racing, however, nothing is certain, everything can change in an instant. Added to the unpredictability of the racing environment and the competing boats is the natural pressure of the clock. The goal: to cross the starting line at just the moment that the starting gun is fired—not a second too early, nor a second too late—and to cross the line with the boat revved up to full speed. Cross the line too soon, and the unlucky boat and its crew will be forced to restart—circling back to the starting line and crossing it again—losing precious time. Cross the line too late—or too slowly—and the competitors can gain an advantage in course position that can't be easily overcome, even by the best crew.

As the countdown to the start reaches its ultimate conclusion, "ten, nine, eight, seven . . ." the crew's hearts are ready to jump out of their chests. Boats that were milling about, almost at random, are now full-bore into their final sprint for the line. At this critical part of a race, teamwork is *everything.* It is essential that skipper and crew communicate with one another flawlessly and work together as one. The best teams at the start are those who can remain calm and collected. More than one race has been won or lost in these critical minutes before the race begins.

And more than one business has lost its own race against the competition before the race has started.

Just What Has Sailboat Racing Got to Do with Business?

When you watch the America's Cup on television, you're seeing the culmination of years of effort. In its infancy, a Cup campaign is a bit like the early days of an entrepreneurial startup business with big plans and little money. As the campaign matures, it takes on the appearance of a high-level research-and-development program. As the actual racing nears, a Cup campaign shares many common features with a professional sports team aimed at a championship. But throughout the whole process is a story that is very similar to almost any medium-sized business facing the competitive pressure of the real world as it strives to bring its product to market, on budget and on time.

For most teams, the early days of a campaign are a

delicate balancing act requiring excellent organizational development, sound planning, and a superb sense of timing. Spend too much of the early money on flashy image-building activities, like warm-up racing and public relations campaigns, and your design effort is sure to fall behind. Pour it all into the design team, and you'll quickly lose your luster in the eyes of potential sponsors and the media. It's an incredibly challenging Catch-22 situation because, without a fast boat, even the best sailors and organizations will fail, and without money, you won't be able to afford your design elements.

In business, it's important to test new products and services *within* the company before they are brought to market. Why? Not only does this process ensure that the new offering will be greeted with open arms by clients and customers but it also keeps the details safe from the prying eyes of the competition. When sailboat racers bring a new boat on-line, they often test it against an established "second" boat with known performance characteristics. The second boat provides the baseline against which the new boat is measured, while ensuring that competitors have a more difficult time gaining intelligence about the new boat's performance envelope. The final result—both in business and in sailboat racing—is a better product, one that will raise the bar against the competition. In business, this means increased revenues and profitability, along with increased customer satisfaction. In sailing, this means faster boat speed, better handling, and more races won. In either case, testing a new boat or product before it "goes to market" can help guarantee that it will be a winner right out of the box.

Once a boat is built (teams are presently allowed to build two new boats per campaign), it is the job of the sailors—working in concert with the design team—to get it up to speed. Hours and hours of testing against a second boat is the tried-and-true method for developing better boat speed. These trials can be employed to test the effect of something as mundane as sail trim, or as radical as a new keel or rudder. Although a boat may show promise when it is first launched, the arduous process of testing can shave valuable seconds—or even minutes—off the boat's time around the racecourse.

But before any boat hits the water, a Cup team must greatly expand its business operations. A waterfront compound must be constructed. Dozens of new employees must be recruited and hired. It takes sixteen people to sail a modern America's Cup boat, and at least an equal number to maintain it shoreside. The recruiting, training, motivation, and retention of a talented team are just as critical to the ultimate success of a sailboat racing effort as they are to *any* business.

Eventually, the clock ticks away to the moment when the business of racing takes a backseat to the racing itself. Once the starting gun sounds, it's up to the skipper and crew to take advantage of all the years of planning, organizing, building, and practice that have enabled them to compete with the best in the world. Although the business of running a sailboat racing team has been left on shore, however, the habits and methods of successful leaders and followers remain. Communication, trust, teamwork, flexibility, perseverance, and numerous other positive business habits and behaviors are just as important during the race as they were in the years leading up to the race, perhaps even more so.

In the end, it's all about whether a team has learned the lessons of sailboat racing, and how skillfully and efficiently the team has harbored and focused its resources. And it's about the courageous men and women who push themselves and their boats to the limits. That is the *true* test of any sailboat racing team—no matter whether its members are sailing a seventy-five-foot boat in the America's Cup, or a sixteen-foot dinghy in a world championship.

Ted Turner: World-Class Sailor and World-Class Businessman

Everything I do is a war.
— TED TURNER

Ted Turner, vice chairman of media giant Time Warner, and founder of the pioneering twenty-four-hour-a-day, all-news cable channel Cable News Network (CNN), will always be known for his brash and daring business style. Whether engineering the $7.6 billion media mega-merger of Turner Broadcasting System with Time Warner, managing his beloved Atlanta Braves baseball team, presiding over a vast portfolio of television networks including CNN, Turner Network Television, TBS SuperStation, and others, pledging $1 billion of his personal wealth to the United Nations, or simply challenging arch-rival Rupert Murdoch to a televised boxing match in Las Vegas, Turner has never been accused of doing anything halfway.

While much of the public are aware of Ted Turner's widely publicized business exploits, many may not know that Turner is also a highly accomplished sailor. In addition to winning the America's Cup in 1977 aboard his boat *Courageous*, Turner has been named Yachtsman of the Year an astounding four times. He accomplished this feat by winning almost every sailing race in sight during the seventies and early eighties in a variety of boats, including the deadly 1979 Fastnet race, a six-hundred-mile ocean race from England, across the Irish Sea, and then back again. In the worst sailboat racing disaster in modern history, fifteen men perished as a Force 10 gale—packing sixty-knot winds, forty-foot waves, and washing-machine seas—pounded the race fleet of 303 boats for twenty hours, knocking more than 100 onto their sides—masts on the water—and completely upending 77 others.

One race in particular, however, stands out as an example of the sheer grit, daring, and talent that Turner can bring to bear to whatever challenge he decides to take on. As part of his campaign to win an unprecedented third Southern Ocean Racing Conference (SORC) victory, Turner sailed his thirty-seven-foot custom sloop, *Lightnin'* in the 1973 Lipton Cup race off the coast of Miami, Florida. As the end of the race drew near—with only three hundred yards to go—Turner's boat was in the lead, but with the second-place boat quickly closing the gap the pressure was on Turner to keeping driving his boat as hard as he possibly could.

Just then, a tugboat towing a huge barge crossed directly in front of *Lightnin'*. The problem wasn't the tugboat or the barge, however, both of which Turner could have easily avoided. The problem was the long steel tow cable strung between the tugboat and the barge, just high enough to cut the mast right off *Lightnin'* if Turner was foolhardy enough to continue on his current heading.

Of course, that's just what Turner did.

As his crew anxiously awaited his order to alter course, Turner—committed to winning the race no matter what the cost—shouted out, "Damn the cable! We're going through!" When the tugboat captain realized that *Lightnin'* was going to do just that, he slowed his boat at the very last second—slackening the cable just enough to allow Turner and his crew to sail over it unharmed.

Victory was his. Again.

Seven Rules to Race By

Why seven rules? Why sailing and business? Why this book?

When we first discussed the idea of merging the two concepts, it seemed like a natural. For Peter Isler—two-time America's Cup winner, television commentator, and owner of Isler Sailing International—sailing has long been a metaphor for life. And for Peter Economy—best-selling business author, longtime manager, and business consultant—the fact that so many men and women sailing at the top levels of the sport were also at the top of the game in business was intriguing, to say the least.

When Isler first broached the idea with some of his fellow sailors at Key West Race Week—a week-long festival of sailboat racing that attracts more than 275 entrants, the reaction was immediate and positive. Whenever Peter brought up the subject, he set off a flood of parallels, rules, and anecdotes supporting and elaborating on the strong links between sailboat racing and business.

In one notable example, George David, chairman and CEO of $25 billion diversified manufacturer United Technologies Corporation of Hartford, Connecticut, explained how he often invokes the "twenty-four-hour rule" in business, a behavior he takes right off the racecourse. "Sailors often call for a one-minute, or five-minute, delay in responding to changed conditions on the race course," he says. "A shift may not last, or a building breeze may drop in velocity, and making big changes in a quick reaction can be costly. The same is true in business, it's often better to take the time to be sure, or to let your judgment season for even the briefest period." A UTC share price five times higher over the last five years just might prove him right.

We listened when four-time America's Cup champion Dennis Conner explained how encouraging your crew to speak up can provide a skipper (or a manager in any organization) with a winning edge over the competition. We listened when Elizabeth Meyer, who lovingly restored the 1930s-vintage America's Cup J-boat *Endeavour*, and who runs a highly successful boat-charter business, described how paying relentless attention to detail can separate the victors from the also-rans. And we listened when Roy Disney, vice chairman of the Walt Disney Company, told us about the importance of having fun, whether sailing on his ocean racer *Pyewacket*, or creating *Fantasia 2000*—Disney's reinvention of the animated classic *Fantasia*.

It was from these candid and insightful interviews—and from our own extensive experience in both sailing and in business—that these rules were forged. As you read through the following rules, think about how you apply them (or *could* apply them) where *you* work.

Rule One—Make a total commitment. Not just the kind of commitment that is easily said, and then just as easily forgotten when the next fire needs to be put out. We're talking about the kind of commitment that runs as deep as the Mississippi River and that is as steady and unchanging as the Rock of Gibraltar—the kind of commitment that your employees, coworkers, and other business partners can rely on fully and without question. It's the kind of commitment that Dennis Conner made when he promised to win the America's Cup back after losing it to Australia in 1983. Four years later, in 1987, he did just that. Not only did Dennis make the initial commitment to win back the Cup, but he backed up his words by making what he calls, a *"commitment to the commitment,"* that is, doing whatever was necessary—from finding the best crew, to raising enough money, to designing and building the best boats, and much, much more—to honor his commitment. Indeed, there's nothing more difficult than beating a competitor who has committed every shred of his or her heart and soul to the fight. The worlds of sailboat racing *and* business are filled with stories of committed underdogs beating out far larger, but less committed competitors—it happens all the time.

Rule Two—Build true team effort. When you're going for the gold in a major sailboat racing campaign, the skipper, the crew, and the entire racing organization absolutely *have* to work together as a team. For Pete du Pont, former governor of Delaware, and current editor of the on-line publication *IntellectualCapital.com,* you build a high-performing team by making *everyone* on the boat an involved part of the crew. For a racing team, there's no other way to win. When you're on a boat surfing along at 25 knots in the middle of the ocean, it feels like you are going 125 knots and there's no place to hide. At that point, anyone who isn't pulling his or her weight becomes quickly and painfully obvious to the rest of the crew. And the results speak for themselves—the racecourse separates the winners from the wannabes.

Any organization, whether it's a grand-prix sailboat racing team or a small, medium, or large business, can build effective teams. All it takes is a commitment from the top to give employees the authority and the autonomy to manage themselves and make the kinds of decisions that have the greatest impact on the team and the support of the organization to encourage and reward true team behavior.

Rule Three—Stack the deck in your favor. In business, and in sailboat racing, you've got to leverage every possible advantage you can in your effort to beat the competition. And make no mistake about it, the goal of both sailboat racing *and* business is to beat the competition—yesterday, today, and tomorrow. According to Chuck Robinson, chairman of the finance committee of shoe-making superstar Nike, and president of the innovative sailboat design company DynaYacht, Inc., tilting the playing field in his favor has brought him tremendous success in business. Consider this simple fact: If you aren't leveraging every possible advantage at your disposal, you can bet your competitors *are*. Winning sailboat racing teams and today's most successful businesses have discovered this simple but powerful lesson. Whether it's staying on the edge of the very latest technological innovations, working harder (or smarter) than the competition, or creating new efficiencies by improving productivity and cutting costs, any advantage you are able to squeeze out of your organization can mean the difference between success and failure.

Rule Four—Be prepared to change course quickly. Sailing and business are both multidimensional activities where change is a constant, and you can be sure that if something hasn't changed lately, it soon will. In fact, the question in today's dynamic global business environment is not *if* things will change, but when, where, and by how much. In the same way, on the racecourse, a shift of wind as small as five degrees can have a dramatic effect on the relative positions of the competitors. In the case of John Thomson, chairman and CEO of Thomson Industries, a producer of precision ball bearings and other industrial and automotive products, an ability to be flexible and to adapt rapidly to change—both on the racecourse, and on the job—have helped him steal victory away from larger and better-funded competitors.

Unfortunately, many organizations—and the men and women who run them—fail to notice fundamental changes in their business environments until it's too late. The danger of that is easily seen in the wreckage of countless organizations that have crashed on the shoals of change. Some companies—for example, IBM when it failed to recognize the long-term significance of the shift of business computing from large, complex, and expensive mainframes to small, simple, and inexpensive personal computers—eventually saw the errors of their ways and were able to save themselves, albeit not without a massive loss of product market share. Today, the best companies can be measured by their ability to change course quickly and decisively in response to changes in their environments.

Rule Five—Expect the unexpected. There's no such thing as being too prepared when it comes to anticipating the kinds of events that can slow down, cripple, or even spell certain death for an organization. In the same way, successful sailboat racing teams consider every possible thing that could ever go wrong in a race—snapped lines, broken electronics, blown sails, an unfavorable wind shift—and develop contingency plans to work around problems in real time, before their boats fall too far behind their competitors. As the earlier example from the 1987 America's Cup Challenger Finals showed, the *Stars & Stripes* team made a dramatic recovery from a blown headsail. If the team hadn't considered just this kind of potentially devastating event in advance, and then intensively trained the crew on how to recover from it, the race's outcome might have been much different.

Rule Six—Push the limits. It's often said that the perfect racing sailboat is one that has pushed the limits of what is humanly and technologically possible so far that it falls apart and sinks just after it wins the regatta. Indeed, there have been more than one or two races where that's exactly what happened, albeit prematurely—including John Bertrand's recent *oneAustralia* America's Cup effort, which you'll read about in Chapter 6. While you certainly don't want your business to fall apart as soon as you achieve *your* goals (or for that matter, *before* you achieve your goals), you do want employees to stretch themselves and to continually push their own personal limits to reach the organization's goals. America's Cup Skipper Dennis Conner talks about "expanding his crew's comfort zone." And at Amway, company president and co-CEO Dick DeVos has built an organization based on a firm foundation of shared values and principles, but where associates are allowed the latitude, creativity, freedom, and initiative to do whatever it takes within that foundation to achieve their dreams and aspirations. When employees push the limits, they are working at their full potential—even expanding that potential! Anything less, and the result is average performance.

Rule Seven—Master the inner game. While having the right equipment and enough time and resources to mount a racing campaign are important steps on the road to winning, there is one more thing that can have just as much of an effect on the ultimate outcome of a race—the state of mind of the participants. Attitude, focus, patience, consistency, and the ability to learn from one's mistakes all play a role in a person's state of mind. An ability to master these elements—the *inner game*—is crucial to long-term success.

Marilyn Wilson-Hadid, vice president of strategic planning and new business development for toymaker Fisher-Price, says that the creation of a learning organization is a critical step in profiting from one's mistakes and building a database of experience that can benefit everyone on the team. It's okay for an employee to make mistakes, but it's not okay for an employee to make a mistake and not learn something from it. And it's *definitely* not okay if the rest of the organization doesn't have the opportunity to learn from it, too.

In each of these chapters, you'll learn the vital lessons that each of these highly successful men and women have learned—in their own words. As you read through these lessons, you'll see how closely sailboat racing and business parallel one another—from the preparation, to the teamwork, to the competition, to any number of other characteristics that the two endeavors share. It's a parallel that the close-knit group of men and women who race sailboats and excel in business feel deep in their bones and apply in their everyday lives, on and off the water—to great success.

And now you can, too.

The Diverse Sport of Sailing

Sailing is truly a great and diverse sport, and—although it costs a lot of money to mount a world-class racing campaign—the casual sailor can get by very inexpensively. There are hundreds of great sailing schools with certified instructors around the country where people can go and learn to sail in a weekend class, and then join a club where they can rent boats as they build their skills—all for less money than a weekend ski trip. The great thing about sailing is its diversity—you can easily sail for a lifetime and still not learn everything there is to know about the sport. There's recreational day sailing, weekend cruising, and ocean passage-making. There are small sailboards and dinghies, open day-sailors, and full-on cruisers to choose from. And you can sail virtually anywhere there is a body of water. But to compete in sailboat racing—at the highest level of the sport—requires a level of commitment that is truly extraordinary.

Chapter Three

Rule One —
Make a Total Commitment

Partway through the 1987 America's Cup campaign, Dennis Conner had a rare meeting with the entire team—shore crew and sailing crew. It took place after dinner one night in the dining room. We were all tired from a long day of training in the blustery winds of the famed "Fremantle Doctor"—the daily sea breeze that blows onto the western coast of Australia from its source in the Indian Ocean—but the fact that Dennis was going to speak to all of us together intrigued every one of the nearly one hundred members of the *Stars & Stripes* team. This had never happened before in the history of the campaign.

What began as simply intriguing turned into one of the most memorable moments of an incredible campaign. Malin Burnham, the chairman of our syndicate, stood before the assembled group and announced that Dennis was going to share something very important—his personal philosophy about competition. After Malin's introduction, Dennis got up and began speaking. As he described his concept of "commitment," you could tell it came from his heart. We were hearing and seeing the real Dennis Conner.

DC explained how we had all unknowingly raised our own comfort level day by day. By training hard—for months on end, in the strong winds and surging ocean off the south coast of Oahu—we had learned to feel *comfortable* sailing a fifty-thousand-pound, 12 Meter sloop in twenty-five knots of wind. Despite the man overboards, the sail blowouts, the broken gear, and even the bruised and battered bodies, we had made real progress. Dennis pointed out that each of us, by making our commitment to the commitment" had worked harder as a group—and together we had raised our own game to the point where we were on the verge of winning the America's Cup. That was not a position any team—no matter *how* talented—could just walk into. It was a result of an awesome team effort made possible by our mutual commitment to the commitment.

With only a hint of a smile, Dennis pointed out this level of intensity is very rare and that he hoped we wouldn't *all* be committed for making the commitment to the commitment! As he spoke, the realization dawned on us—that he was absolutely right. It was all about our comfort level. You read stories about people doing incredible things—lifting cars off babies, and similar superhuman feats—but nobody can perform at that high level day in and day out (as we had to during the grueling four months of trials in Australia). A year before, none of us would have been comfortable being in the position we were in, closing in on a historic victory. Our own standards—the bar by which we measure our daily activities—had indeed been raised. And we were all the better for it.

What does it mean to be committed to something or to someone? Is commitment situational—subject to whatever course of action is most expedient at any given moment? Does it ebb and flow like a fast-running tide, or is it built on a stronger foundation, something that is deeper and longer lasting? Are words enough, or can commitment truly be measured only through the actions of those who practice it?

When we surveyed our group, the message came through loud and clear: success in sailboat racing *and* in business can be measured by the depth of one's commitment to winning. It's not just about being focused on crossing the finish line ahead of the competition—it runs *much* deeper than that. Commitment involves all those "little things," too: paying attention to every critical detail, insisting on quality, practicing before you perform, and refusing to give up—no matter how difficult the circumstances or how uncertain the outcome.

In this chapter, we'll focus on all the things that add up to the "Big C"—commitment—and we'll discover what today's most successful businesspeople do to put their words into action.

Make a Commitment to the Commitment

If there is one person in the sport of sailboat racing who most personifies the word commitment, it is Dennis Conner. Dennis, who has sailed in a record eight America's Cup campaigns—winning it four times—is without a doubt one of the world's most accomplished sailors. He has committed himself, his money, and his organization countless times over the years to compete in and win at the highest, most challenging level of the sport.

Dennis's commitment is so strong that, even when handicapped by a slow boat—as in the 1995 America's Cup campaign—or by a crew that is not as talented as its competitors, he can bring out the best in himself and in his crew, and win through sheer force of will.

In his book *The Art of Winning*, Dennis explains the power of commitment:

* Commitment puts order in your life.
* It establishes values.
* It sets your priorities.
* It tests all the skills you've got.
* Commitment makes everything you're doing worthwhile.

When explaining exactly what it is about making a commitment to winning that increases your chances of doing just that, he observes, "Commitment allows you to make the effort to operate at a very high level of your ability. And then, after that happens, your self-image changes and you can operate at an even higher level than you could have beforehand." As Dennis Conner describes it, commitment goes far deeper than the simple act of making a commitment. When you make a commitment, and then take action to fulfill your commitment, you actually make a physiological and psychological change within yourself. What was once impossible is now possible. When a man's or a woman's commitment is strong enough, there is nothing that can stand in his or her way—*nothing*.

Commitment doesn't just happen in an organization. While some employees who feel they have a direct stake in the organization may have unlimited commitment, others may not. According to Dick Watts, president and CEO of enterprise data storage manufacturer ConvergeNet Technologies, Inc., of San Jose, California, the trick is to build a culture of commitment that involves everyone in the organization, regardless of position on the organizational chart. "The word commitment definitely comes to mind when I think about a successful organization. When you build a value system for a company—whatever that value system is—you want the people in the organization to buy into it. You can't have everybody operating at cross-purposes. So when you're building a culture, you want people to understand it, but also to commit to living by those rules. And it also has to have a really strong self-reinforcing aspect. If the leadership team really lives by those rules, then I think it gets a lot easier for the rest of the organization to fall into line and you have a stronger team.

"There's no doubt that a significant factor in our team winning the San Francisco J-105-class season championship last year was that we were there at every race. Some of our competitors missed a few races and those became their throw-outs. That helped us when it came to the end of the year. While we didn't have all the same people on board week in and week out, we did have the same core team. The fact is, that level of commitment on our part—my partner Tom and I—to making sure the boat was fitted out properly, that we had taken care of cleaning the bottom and so on, to doing the things that we were accountable for and then expecting the same of the crew all really helped. It's one of the values we established early on; a high level of commitment is one thing that really makes a difference, so let's all sign up early on to do that. We did, and we won."

The power of commitment is real, and it can make a tremendous difference in your work life.

Pay Relentless Attention to Detail

In business, as in life, it seems that some of us are detail people, and some of us aren't. You know the folks who are detail-oriented—they're the ones who get started on their projects well before they are due. In staff meetings, they always seem to have the answers to all the questions and, if they don't, you can be sure that they'll get them as soon as the meeting adjourns—perhaps sooner. They let no work leave their hands until every single little detail has been examined, every consequence tracked to its ultimate conclusion, every "i" dotted, and every "t" crossed.

While some of us may cringe at the thought of having to worry about this level of detail—maybe we see ourselves as "big-picture" people—others live to do just that. And their attention to detail has given them a leg up on their peers—and their competition.

Several members of our group weighed in very strongly on this particular point.

For Elizabeth Meyer, founder and CEO of the International Yacht Restoration School in Newport, Rhode Island, and president of J-Class Management, also of Newport, it's not enough to simply pay attention to detail, you have to pay *relentless* attention to detail if you are going to achieve your most challenging goals.

And Elizabeth should know. When she was only three years old, she would sit in the bilge of her family's Star-class sailboat with two stuffed animals and listen as her mother told her stories of the fabled J-boats racing in America's Cup competition off Newport. Built from the late 1920s to 1937, the J-boats—with their 130-foot hulls, thirty-two-member crews, and stalwart names like *Enterprise, Resolute*, and *Ranger*—are considered by many to be the most beautiful sailboats ever created. Unfortunately, of the ten J-boats originally built, all but three were scrapped during World War II.

In 1983, Elizabeth chanced upon the rusted-out hull of perhaps the most fabled J-boat of them all, *Endeavour*, in a boatyard in the south of England. *Endeavour* was built and skippered by well-known British aviator T. O. M. Sopwith (of Sopwith Camel fame), and it nearly won the America's

Cup in 1934. Elizabeth bought the derelict hull and moved it lock, stock, and barrel to Calshot Spit, an abandoned seaplane base on the English coast—her new home for the next five years. With a loving attention to detail, Elizabeth Meyer restored *Endeavour* to her former glory, and then some. Today the boat sails the world, and turns heads in every harbor she appears in.

Says Meyer, "I see strong similarities between managing a big project or a business, and setting up a boat for a sailboat race. For both, you are keeping track of a million details and every single one of them is vitally important. It's your capacity to be relentless in your attention to detail that is a major part of succeeding or not succeeding."

Dick DeVos, president and co-CEO of Amway Corporation, based in Ada, Michigan, has found tremendous success, both on and off the water. DeVos, who campaigns his One Design 48 sloop *Windquest*, manages to stay near the top of his class in whatever events he enters. DeVos attributes much of his success to paying attention to detail.

"On a boat, I bring a little bit of an intensity and a focus on detail. I'm not someone who is an outrageous or loud personality, some of whom run in sailing circles. I simply try to do the little things right."

Jack Woodhull, former chairman and CEO of Logicon, Inc., a defense contractor that is now a subsidiary of Northrop Grumman, is also a big believer in paying attention to detail.

"You should pay attention to detail—in business and in sailing. You have to validate everything you're doing. You have to check and double check—that's a very important aspect of business. You just can't check enough. Somebody writes a contract, and if the CEO doesn't read that contract, he's going to find himself in hot water sooner or later."

If you're already detail-oriented, then you're already ahead of the game. However, if you're not, then make paying attention to detail a part of your plan for success. It *will* pay off for you—*guaranteed*.

Every Little Bit Helps

On even the smallest boat, attention to detail is incredibly important. To give you an idea of the level of detail we're talking about, here is a sample checklist for a sailor preparing to race his or her thirteen-foot-long Laser dinghy. One sail, one sailor: all Lasers come out of the same mold, and are virtually identical.

* Inspect all high-load areas, ropes, and fittings (of which there are very few).
* Drain all water out of hull—every last drop.
* Make sure hull is completely clean—wipe down with acetone.
* Make sure the sail is perfectly aligned at the top of the mast.
* Don't let the sail flap—it decreases the life of the sail by making it stretchier.
* Ensure clothing is as light as possible for the given conditions.
* Keep centerboard and rudder fins covered to avoid scratches until it is time to launch the boat.

✳ Don't launch the boat until the last possible minute to keep the hull from absorbing water.

✳ Make sure you have the latest weather forecast—log on to the Internet right before leaving the dock to obtain the latest forecast and wind readings from nearby weather buoys.

✳ Do a full range of stretches before leaving shore and stretch more before the race.

✳ Schedule your morning so that you can be one of the first boats to set sail for the racecourse (psych factor + preparation time).

✳ Look at the scoreboard and record the point totals of nearby competitors (if this is a multiday regatta).

✳ Look at the notice board to see if there have been any changes made to sailing instructions.

✳ Lather up with sunscreen, etc. etc.

You get the idea. All of these activities occur *before* the sailor even leaves the dock. Some of these points may have an effect that is hard to measure, I mean, how much water does a fiberglass hull absorb when immersed for fifteen minutes longer in the water? Others can mean the difference between a first place and a disqualification, for example, if some key aspect of the sailing instructions has been changed (like the location of the turning marks). But it all adds up. Racers learn to be detail-oriented because, in sailboat racing, you are *always* striving for even the slightest edge on the competition. If you feel that you are more prepared (by attending to all the little details) than your competitors, you will create a psychological advantage that can set the tone for your entire day. Confidence breeds success.

As Roy Disney says, "The devil is in the details."

Insist on Quality

As they say at the Ford Motor Company, "Quality Is Job One." Commitment can be expressed in many different ways. One of the most obvious ways to express commitment is to do whatever it takes to produce a quality product, deliver a quality service, or give a quality performance. By refusing to settle for less than the best from yourself and others, your commitment will find physical expression.

When Elizabeth Meyer restored the America's Cup J-boat *Endeavour*, she wasn't about to do the job halfway. This boat deserved the best, and that's what she got. Says Meyer, "I insisted on quality, no matter what it took to get it. I was willing to suffer a lot and have people dislike me a lot to get the boat the way I wanted it. I just won't put up with work that isn't really good. I know that people are capable of really good work and I make them do it. And sometimes they end up liking me, but a lot of times they don't, and I don't care."

And you can't argue with the result. *Endeavour* is a sailing work of art—and she is also a business. *Endeavour* and *Shamrock V,* another America's Cup J-boat from the 1930s, are both available for charter from J-Class Management. Here's a description of *Endeavour*'s interior excerpted from the J-Class Management Web site (www.jclass.com). As you'll see, the quality of Elizabeth's work drips from every word used to describe the boat. Keep in mind that when Elizabeth found the boat, it was a rusting hulk that couldn't even float!

> Belowdecks, *Endeavour* has the air of an Edwardian men's club. She is finished in raised panels of American cherry with a satin luster. The solid wood paneling is set off by beveled glass, nickel and platinum plated fixtures and tapestry-weave wool, cotton and silk fabrics. . . . *Endeavour*'s interior avoids the darkness of most flush-deck yachts through the use of myriad skylights and "juice-squeezer" deck prisms. . . . The interior layout provides accommodation for eight charter guests in four staterooms—two with queen size berths, one with a king size berth and one with twin berths. The staterooms adjoin baths with nickel plated shower enclosures and heated towel bars. The master bath has an oversize tub. Forward of the staterooms is a 22′ by 14′ salon and dining area, complete with a fully operational marble fireplace, a solid cherry dining table, full bar hidden behind false book bindings and the usual entertainment systems. Forward of the salon are the restaurant-standard galley, laundry and crew's quarters from which the captain and crew provide first-class food and service. Altogether, *Endeavour*'s interior furnishes a beautiful, elegant and comfortable counterpoint to the sailing excitement on deck.

As Chuck Robinson, chairman of the finance committee of the board of directors of shoemaker Nike Corporation, and president of high-tech sailboat design firm DynaYacht, Inc., says, "If it's worth doing, then do it the best you can do it." Indeed if you're not willing to commit yourself to producing the best product possible, or providing your customers with the highest levels of service, or learning and growing within your chosen vocation or profession, then why bother at all?

Your work is a direct reflection of you as a person. Always give it your very best. Whether you succeed or fail, by making the commitment to produce the highest-quality products and services, you're making a commitment to yourself, to your coworkers, to your organization, and to your customers and clients.

Practice, Practice, Practice

You've heard the old saying, practice makes perfect. And while you might intuitively know that the old saying is true, have you ever put it into practice—*really* put it into practice on the job? The simple fact is that the more you practice something—whether it's drafting performance appraisals, performing a routine technical task, making a presentation to management, asking for a raise, or any of the many other things that we do in our business lives—the better you'll get at doing it. And the better you get at doing something, the more effective you'll be, and the more often you'll be successful in any given endeavor.

According to Malin Burnham, chairman of the board of

John Burnham & Company, practice is critical to winning sailboat races. "In any big race or series I've ever gone to, I don't go out without practicing. Hours and hours and hours of practicing. In fact, the basic rule of thumb is five to ten hours of practice for every hour spent on the racecourse."

Elizabeth Meyer agrees. "Once you've got the right people and you've made sure that they know exactly what you want of them, then you have to practice and practice and practice and practice until jibing and tacking is second nature. When you have that, you have the tools to go out on the water and win."

If you're getting ready to make a business presentation, prepare it ahead of time, and then rehearse it again and again—refining your script and your visual aids as you go. If you're really brave, you can invite a trusted colleague in to watch and offer his or her feedback. Similarly, if you're preparing a pitch to your boss to get a raise or promotion, run through it several times in advance. Take time to anticipate every possible objection, and prepare responses to counter them.

Practice really *does* make perfect. Give it a try the next time you have a performance to make and see what it does for you.

Never Give Up!

What is it that causes people to pursue their goals against what seem like insurmountable odds? What is it about the nature and depth of their commitment that separates the winners in an organization from the also-rans? While some people are incredibly talented and smart, it takes more than smarts to succeed in life. All the smarts in the world aren't going to make the least bit of difference in the world if they aren't applied.

North Marine Group president Tom Whidden's philosophy on winning is very clear and unambiguous: "I never let up. Ever, ever—never! I hate to lose. And what I really hate about it is that it takes exactly the same effort to lose as it does to win. So, if you're going to make that effort, why not make the effort to win?" Perhaps that's one reason why Tom has won three America's Cups, and why he has grown his organization into the largest sail company in the world.

Thomson Industries' John Thomson has also learned the power of refusing to give up over and over again. He has seen the power of perseverance work in his business, and he has seen it work on the water. In business, John was particularly proud when his relatively small company beat out more than one hundred others—some many times the size of Thomson Industries—to acquire the actuator product group from General Motors in 1987. The acquisition didn't happen overnight—it took months and months of hard work. And it wasn't easy—other companies tried to push the deal off track, and dealing with GM's bureaucracy turned into a test of its own. But throughout it all, John Thomson and his team refused to give up. The result was victory when the sale was completed, and Thomson Industries was able to successfully integrate the product group into its business.

Says Thomson, "We were trying to buy the group from

General Motors and we had heard rumors that they were going to try to spin it off. I decided to write to the chairman of General Motors and ask him if this was in fact true. Eight months later we got a call from a large New York investment banking firm saying that the product group was going to be spun off by GM and asking if we were interested in a package.

"We got the package and found out that we were one of about one hundred companies that had expressed interest in buying it—from Fortune 10 companies, to small, private entities. We knew we weren't going to win in a bidding war, but we put our team together and had the patience to work with GM, which was frustrating at times. But we waited it out, and people dropped out along the way, or got eliminated by GM or by Solomon Brothers. It took close to ten months to negotiate the contract and finalize the deal.

"During the last week of the acquisition process, a Fortune 10 company tried to pressure GM into selling to them. They were obviously trying to intrigue GM with more cash. But GM said no, they thought we were the right fit. Patience—and our refusal to give up—paid off.

"So my advice is this: Never, ever give up—ever! At GM, no one would have ever, ever suspected that this little company named Thomson Industries would have won this thing. If you had to rank the one hundred companies competing for the product group by size, we were probably in the bottom fifty. But we refused to give up. It was a great learning opportunity for me—all of the lessons from sailing definitely applied—and, as it turned out, it was a wonderful experience."

Jay Ecklund's Secrets of Success

J ay Ecklund, former chairman of Young America Corporation, the Minnesota-based rebate-and-coupon fulfillment house, has a long history of winning—both in business and on the sailboat racecourse. In 1997, Ecklund sold his company to BT Capital Partners, Inc., for an undisclosed amount, reported by the media to be in the neighborhood of $100 million. Ecklund bought Young America Corporation in 1975, and grew the company from 19 employees and about $400,000 in annual sales to the top of its industry, with $150 million in annual sales and some 1,500 employees. While preparing to collect the Governor's Trophy at the 1999 Acura SORC in Miami Beach, Florida, for his boat *Starlight,* Jay revealed some of his secrets of success—in sailing and in business:

* If you can't find a way, force your way.
* Protect your flanks while attacking.
* Be outcome driven within the rules.

Chapter Four

Rule Two —
Build True Team Effort

On a two-person dinghy, like the sixteen-foot, Olympic 470–class sailboat that Peter Isler's wife, J J, races, the skipper—J J—and her crew—Pease Glaser—operate as a team on a variety of levels. Simply keeping the boat upright can be a big challenge when the wind picks up over twenty knots—with Pease standing balanced on the edge of the boat, hanging in a harness from a thin metal wire (called, appropriately, a "trapeze"), while J J sits leaning out as far as possible over the edge to keep the boat from being flipped over by the force of the wind. In very light winds, both must move gingerly, like cats, to avoid shaking the precious wind from the sails. In fresh breezes, they literally have to "muscle" the boat around the course, pumping their body weight aggressively to propel the boat through maneuvers. That's when sailing a lightweight dinghy like a 470 becomes more fun than any carnival ride.

The mental and physical responsibilities are divided up according to each of their skills and their position on the boat. The skipper, J J, concentrates on boat speed—picking the best path through the waves—and the positioning of the boat at the mark roundings and when other boats come near. In addition to balancing the boat as the wind and waves push and pull on the craft, Pease keeps an eye on the big picture—the shifts and puffs of wind—and develops the overall strategy for the race, relaying it to J J from her precarious perch on the side of the boat.

Experience has shown that there is no one "right" way to divide up the responsibilities aboard a 470. While there are a few hard and fast rules—the skipper drives and the crew hangs from the trapeze—the top teams vying for honors in this highly competitive international class develop their own system after sailing together for some time and the best teams are constantly striving for refinements to their personal system. The rewards? A world championship, or an Olympic Gold medal is the ultimate prize. And as every 470 sailor knows, the crew gets the same size medal as the skipper—these sailors really know that it is a team effort!

Teams have been a hot topic in business for some time

now. Just how hot? A quick search of Amazon.com shows more than 250 business books with the word "team" in the title. *That's* hot! And if you haven't already been to some sort of team-building workshop or event at work (or two or three), you can bet you soon will be. Instead of the usual business fads that come crashing into organizations out of nowhere, and then disappear just as quickly, the idea of team building has real staying power.

Of course, there's a reason for that.

The reason is because teams *really* do make a difference. Each and every one of us has had this formula drilled into us from a very young age: 1 + 1 = 2. That may be true in a strict, mathematical sense, but with the application of team-work in an organization, 1 + 1 can equal far more than 2. When people work together to achieve a common goal, the result is often *far* more than the sum of its parts.

In many ways, the different positions within a sailboat racing team mirror the positions within a typical company. It's a small world, after all.

Helmsman = Chairman. The helmsman sets the overall vision for the boat and is responsible for steering it. In many organizations, the chairman is responsible for creating a vision and communicating it to his or her management team and other employees.

Tactician = CEO. The tactician is responsible for dealing with boat-to-boat challenges and looking for opportunities such as puffs of wind to exploit. Similarly, a company's CEO is responsible for day-to-day operations and for executing plans to achieve the company's vision and goals while keeping an eye to the horizon, always alert for new opportunities.

Navigator = CFO. The navigator monitors the boat's performance by looking at the conditions on the racecourse and by monitoring data output from onboard computers and instruments. The CFO monitors data from accounting and management information systems to ensure that the organization's performance is at desired levels.

These first three positions comprise the "afterguard" on a sailboat, and the top management team in many organizations.

Mainsail trimmer = Sales manager. The mainsail trimmer is a key member of the speed team—responsible for constantly adjusting and optimizing the shape of the main sail. He also provides a communication link between the other sail trimmers and the afterguard. In this role, the mainsail trimmer works to capture puffs of wind that the afterguard has steered the boat to be in position to exploit, just as a sales manager works with top management to position the company's products and services before key clients and customers.

Sail trimmers/Speed team = Sales force. Sail trimmers are responsible for optimizing the trim of the sails to generate the most boat speed. In the same way, a company's sales force balances the organization's resources to garner the maximum return in terms of sales and profitability. The overall market is like the prevailing wind on the racecourse, and a puff of wind is like an individual customer requiring quick reactions by the trimmers or sales force.

Grinders = Sales support team. Acting on the instruction of the sail trimmers, grinders use their strength to turn the winches that retrim the sails. A sales support team takes care of all the administrative details that allow a company's sales force to focus on their number-one job: *selling*.

Bow, Pit, and Mast Man. In an organization, these are the regular workers—the people who produce and deliver the company's products and services and administer its processes and systems under the direction of management. This is just like the Bow, Pit, and Mast Man who takes commands from the afterguard to hoist, drop, and change sails, and do the physical work and other routine things that need to be done so that the boat can sail around the racecourse. Practice, teamwork, timing and communication are all critical to proper job performance.

Get the Right People

Building an effective team starts with recruiting the right people. Notice that we said the *right* people—not necessarily the smartest people, or the ones with the longest résumé, or the ones with the biggest egos. Every organization is different, based on a unique set of values, missions, and goals.

Because of these differences, there is no one person that is the best fit for *every* organization—instead, some people are right for a particular organization, while others are definitely wrong and fit better elsewhere.

The trick is to clearly identify the values, missions, and goals that your organization holds dear, and then translate them into yardsticks with which you can measure potential new members. To that end, it's critically important that you look at each recruit in as unbiased a manner as you possibly can. One way to do this is to involve other members of your team in the interview and selection process. Ask your candidate to spend a day at your organization, meeting and greeting the members of the team and getting to know them. After each interview, ask your employees to give their candid feedback and use it to stack up the candidates.

John Bertrand, winner of the 1983 America's Cup, veteran of five America's Cup campaigns, and cofounder and vice chairman of Quokka Sports, has seen firsthand the importance of hiring the right people—particularly in a fast-moving, Internet start-up that is poised to take the world of sports media by storm. "In the world of start-ups, you can't be concerned about the consequences of failure. One has to live the dream and get people who are willing to do that, who are also comfortable in living on the edge. The key is to hire up—we call it Quokka DNA—to endeavor to hire people better than ourselves so that we work ourselves out of a job. To do that requires a lot of self-confidence, of course, but it's a very, very important cultural value within our company. Why? Because we know the power of great people. We know this from this sport of yacht racing. You get great talent on the boat, and if somehow you can allow that chemistry to work such that $1 + 1 = 3$, then you can move mountains.

"I once asked Lowell North how he recruited the people to build North Sails in the early days. He said, 'Anyone who can beat me out on the racetrack I try and hire. Not only do they have the required skills in terms of tactics and boat speed but they also have to have the ability to organize themselves, organize their boats, organize crews, and organize money—that is, to pull together campaigns to be able to beat me because I'm pretty good at what I do.' "

Jack Woodhull, former chairman of Logicon, Inc., believes that getting the right people for your team should be at the top of any manager's list of things to do. According to Woodhull, "In business you don't succeed if you don't have good people who can get along and who are responsible. The same thing is true in sailboat racing. You have to get good people and you have to mold them into a team, or they have to be willing to be part of an existing team. Plus, they have to be smart and they have to be responsible. The better the people are, the more likely you are to win."

And it's important to understand that it may take some adjustments in assignments before you hit on the winning combination. Woodhull continues, "You're never a hundred percent successful right out of the starting box. You may have to keep changing things until you finally get the right people in the right slot. That's true in business and it's true in sailing."

Building a successful, highly motivated team takes more than simply running a want ad, wading through a stack of résumés, and hiring a bunch of eager new recruits. Your organization's culture—and the actions of its managers—

will determine whether true team effort will flourish or die. Are employee-run teams encouraged or discouraged? Are employee teams run by managers, or by the employees who are on the front line—the employees who know what needs to be done? Does management trust employees to do the right thing, and leave them alone to do just that?

Amway Corporation has a very strong corporate culture, built on a foundation of entrepreneurship, fair play, family values, service to community, and independence. Since its very beginnings in 1959, company founders Rich DeVos and Jay Van Andel sought to create an organization that would allow people to dream big dreams, and to give them the tools to make their dreams reality. Because of Amway's strong culture, it's particularly important that potential team members fit into the culture, rather than the culture trying to fit to the candidate.

According to Amway president and co-CEO Dick DeVos, son of company cofounder Rich DeVos, "We're a business that tries to reflect a set of core values. What we try to do is foster an entrepreneurial spirit within the organization and yet to do that inside the construct of a defined set of values and principles. Within that framework, we want people to have the ability to get creative and to be innovative. Certainly our Amway distributor population needs very little encouragement to be innovative. They tend to be highly entrepreneurial."

An organization's values serve not only as milestones by which employees can measure their own behavior but they also delineate the boundaries of acceptable employee behavior. All employees need to know the rules of the game, and the standards by which they will be judged when it's time for managers to appraise their performance.

Says DeVos, "Management expert Ken Blanchard has a great metaphor: A river without banks is nothing but a big puddle. You have to have boundaries if you're going to be able to direct the flow—and shared values comprise those boundaries. We spend a lot of time talking to people to make sure they are comfortable with our philosophy. If you're not, then, frankly, you're not going to be happy here. And that's okay. You don't have to agree with us philosophically. You don't have to agree with our view of life, but if you don't you probably don't want to work here.

"A group of great sailors doesn't necessarily make a great *team* of sailors. There have to be some principles around which you coalesce—when you're on a boat in close proximity, that becomes evident—maybe even quicker than in a business. We'd rather sail with a good group of people that we know and enjoy and connect with, rather than a passing parade of whoever seems to be the hottest one in town. At the end of the day, not only the tangible but the intangible results are much better. The tangible result is that you win on the racecourse. But the intangible result is the joy factor. It is so much higher when you're working effectively with a group that you enjoy being with and that you line up with philosophically."

Dennis Conner is always on the lookout for the best people to join his teams. One of his favorite sayings is that winning races is all about "Staffing, staffing, and staffing!" When he is not embroiled in a full-scale campaign, Dennis keeps his skills sharp by sailing frequently, and in all sorts of races, in all kinds of places. This means that he sails with crews of differing levels of experience and depth of commitment. Through experience, Dennis has become an expert at quickly assessing the talents—and the limits—of the members of his crew, and adjusting his expectations and demands on them accordingly. He has an uncanny ability, which is the hallmark of a great leader, to get the best out of just about anyone—no matter what their level or experience.

Says Dennis, "I know the people I have and I have a pretty good idea of their skill level, so I don't try to operate the boat beyond that level. Sometimes in a low-key weekend race I'll have guys on board who are just barely capable of getting the sail up and down. If that's the case, then I don't try to jibe-set at the weather mark—we'll simply put the sail up and then, once it is flying and everyone is ready, we'll jibe."

This is a valuable lesson to anyone wanting to get peak performance out of their organization. It's a simple fact of life that sometimes we won't have the most talented or experienced person in every position on the crew. Like Dennis, we should know our team well enough so that we don't ask its members to operate beyond their limits. That's the beauty of a team effort—we can still win the race despite our individual shortcomings.

George David, chairman and CEO of United Technologies, knows that the strength of an organization reflects the skill sets and motivation of its key people, and also how well they know each other and work together. He believes the organization's leaders have to be involved personally in recruiting and developing future generations of employees and managers, and sets an example himself with hands-on involvement in the process, recruiting on a half dozen campuses each year. He also believes in giving a management team enough time to become mature in their knowledge of their business and in their relationships with each other.

Says George, "The most important thing we do in business is develop future generations of employees and executives. It's also the longest cycle single thing we do. Think about it, the typical R&D program has a two- to five-year span, employee development at the more senior levels can be three to four times longer. This is the biggest bang in business, it's also the slowest bang." Speaking about UTC, he says, "The strength of this organization actually reflects decisions I made about people fifteen or twenty years ago.

"The same thing is true in sailing. Most of my relationships in sailing go back a long time. A big part of the success of the *Idler* program (David's racing boats have all been named after a Samuel Johnson essay) has been the behind the scenes influence of people like Tom Whidden, Tom McLaughlin, and Bruce Nelson. Most of the people who sail with me have been steady crew members for a decade.

"Here's the best way to be persuasive about this," he says. "Put any new crewman on a fifty-footer, where the rail gets congested, and he's almost sure to get an elbow in the face the first tack or two or three. There's choreography in how these boats and their crews go side to side, everything happens fast, and each of us learns the peculiarities of the others. The same is true in business, you just have to learn how the enterprise works and how its key people fit and work together.

"Another reason to be careful with change is that each

person brings his own initiatives and ideas. We always benefit from these, and constant but controlled insertion of new
talent is always needed. But, especially in business and at the
more senior levels, change is always a re-start and thus has
its own burden: all clocks go to zero, every program gets re-
baselined, every budget gets reset. You can't let the loss of
corporate memory become the excuse for a new day. Momentum, especially in big enterprises, counts—and counts
for lots."

Robert Hughes

Owner, Advantage Benefits Group

As the owner of a One Design 35 and a Melges 24 named
Heartbreaker, my career and company have been deeply in-
fluenced by the sport of competitive sailing since I began in
1986. Even my company's new logo resembles a reflection of
a sailboat in a large *A* for Advantage Benefits Group. Our
firm helps employers all over the Midwest with their employee benefits programs (401k plans, pension plans, health,
life, disability, etc.).

I started as a novice racer and quickly learned some
traits that applied equally to business success and winning
sailboat races. Learn from the best by sailing and doing
work with the best. Get better by competing against the
best. If you want to be better in your career or as a sailor you
might as well compete against the Michael Jordans of the
world. Sailing allows you to do that and can give you the
confidence to go after certain business projects you may have
lacked the confidence for before. Team building (whether

it's getting crew to help sand the bottom of a boat, hike for twenty-four hours on a distance race, motivation, and working toward a common goal) really carries over to business. Many sailors want the glory positions in the afterguard, same in business; motivating the troops at all levels—grinders, receptionist—is a challenge you learn from sailing. Crew preparation, making sure you have the right equipment, spending the necessary funds, living with your budget, same as business. There is a time you need to spend money to make money in business, just as when it is time to buy new sails. In picking the right key employees and crew, you need to know what to look for, including dedication, skills, commitment, and most important, a great *attitude*! We are not great alone, but only as a team, and we are only as good as our weakest link. A bad mast man can make a great bowman look bad, a bad service department can make a great salesman look bad! Organization, logistics, responsibilities, etc.—whether running your company or a grandprix campaign, you will go nowhere without them!

Putting together a successful company and keeping it on track is very similar to keeping a winning boat program going—getting the right people, practice, motivation, taking care of those people so they stay with you, and filling the holes when you lose them. Racing has also opened a lot of doors for us by introducing us to people we would have not normally met. And our winning program has certainly given us some great local press, helping with identity. As part of my work, I do a lot of employee meetings for companies to explain their benefits and to get the employees to buy into the program—much like getting the crew to buy into the weekend practice we need to do. Many times I can use some good sailing stories to make the meetings more enjoyable. Finally, coming full circle, after we sold our last company to a local bank, sailing helped give me the confidence to start a new company, ABG, and my sailing connections allowed me to pursue a dream of creating a new one design boat, fast, portable, fun to sail—inshore and off—and affordable! The One Design 35! I'm very proud of how my vision has excited forty other owners so far! Getting the designer, builder, and other investors together has been a great learning project! Our success on the racecourse has translated to our success in our industry, and in many ways they go hand in hand!

Communicate (But Mostly Listen)

Information is power, but even the most valuable information is worthless if it isn't communicated efficiently, clearly, and to the right people. Communication is the lifeblood of any organization, and its free and unfettered flow marks the best organizations and sets them apart from those that have yet to reach the front of the pack.

But in the hustle and bustle of our busy lives at work, many of us forget that communication is a two-way street. Despite its importance, listening is one skill that many of us find it all too easy to neglect. Being on the receiving end of communication is just as important as being on the sending end, however. The best communication is not just from boss to subordinate, it's up, down, and across the organization.

As anyone in business knows, good communication doesn't just happen. It takes the concerted and ongoing efforts of *everyone* in an organization to create and sustain it. Knowing this, the best leaders encourage the members of their team to speak up. They are aware that good ideas can be found anywhere, and that the team that has the best and most complete information is the team that has the best chance of winning on any given day.

So even when Dennis Conner is pretty sure he already knows the answer, he asks his crew anyway. He knows from experience that encouraging his crew to speak up can benefit the organization tremendously. According to Dennis, "Ninety-nine percent of the time when I ask a question, I already know the answer. But when I ask, 'Which way should we go, what should we do, or, do we need to change sails?' I am getting my crew to think on their own. If they can't quite sort out the answer, I'll give them hints such as, 'What about those guys up there? Are they higher or lower— what's going on?' This is to let them learn—to lead them to the right answer. I do this because the other one percent of the time when I *don't* know the answer, I will need their help. But if they are not accustomed to giving input, then they won't be ready to help—or they'll be afraid to speak up. The worst thing you can do is to belittle them or make fun of their input in front of their peers—then they'll be hesitant to speak in the future. So, if you want their help—if you really *do* want their help—then make them feel good about being there by listening to what they have to say."

But can there be too much of a good thing? What if your employees think they need to chime in with their ideas all at the same time? North Sails' Tom Whidden believes that it's better to have more information than less, and he illustrates his belief with an anecdote about his longtime sailing partner Dennis Conner. "Dennis is really good about having the whole crew speak up—even if there are eleven guys or more on the boat, and no matter how far down the ranks you go. Even at a key time when he's one hundred percent focused on an issue. Dennis knows that the worst that could happen is that maybe he'll get too much knowledge all at once, but that doesn't bother a mature person who's been there and has a lot of experience. He just tunes out what's not important, and tunes in what *is* important."

Not everyone is a Dennis Conner, able to process an unlimited stream of input during moments of high pressure. I know that would just distract me when *I* am driving a boat. Nevertheless, I still want to find a way to make everyone feel involved and have the feeling that their insight is valued. That's where postrace team meetings can provide a valuable forum for discussing ideas. While racing, however, I'll assign certain crew members to be responsible for discrete areas—tactics, boat speed, boat handling, and so forth. So if someone on the crew wants to give their input, they can address it to the appropriate person. Then, if it's deemed that the information is important enough for me to get it, the appropriate crew member will forward it to me. Otherwise it will be filtered out so that I (and other members of the team) am not distracted. But everyone on the boat knows that if they see something really important ("Hey, do you see that boat about to hit us?!"), they can just yell it out!

Putting together a full-length animated feature film involves an incredible team effort. From inception, to the drawing and painting of storyboards and *thousands* of cels, to the distribution and promotion of the final product—and everything else in between—it's a team effort from beginning to end. If anyone understands the impact of teamwork on a film, and on an organization, Roy Disney, vice chairman of the Walt Disney Company, certainly does.

To Roy, teams are an essential element in business. And teams are also a critical element on his extremely successful racing series of sailboats named *Pyewacket*. During the design process for Roy's newest *Pyewacket*—a seventy-two-foot maxi-sled—Disney had regular team meetings. Every detail of the boat, from the galley to the height of the winches, was carefully analyzed—not just by the designer and Roy but by the entire crew. This sort of team involvement is very rare, and it highlights Disney's respect for his entire team. The results—which include most of the West Coast's elapsed time records in offshore races—speak for themselves.

Disney says, "I've always believed in equality of opportunity in terms of teamwork. And that's true on a boat, as well as in business. On *Pyewacket*, we always have team meetings and everyone is encouraged to contribute. Sometimes the guy on the bow knows more about what's going on up there than you do in the back steering the boat. There's an old story about Walt from the early days when we were making short subjects—really just a collection of gags. Every week, Walt had a gag contest and everybody was free to enter—the winner got five dollars, which was a lot of money during the Depression. And who kept winning, week after week? The janitor. You see, it's not about who's the boss. It's about who's got the best ideas."

That's what listening to your employees is really all about—getting the best ideas. Says Pete du Pont, "You've got to recognize that you may be the skipper and you may own the boat, but that doesn't mean you're the smartest person in the world. It pays to let your crew talk to you and to listen to what they have to say because they're able people too, and they'll see things and have recommendations that may be right on. You've got to let them talk and you've got to listen. Then the trick is to separate the wheat from the chaff, pick the good ideas, and discard the ones that aren't so good."

Fisher-Price's Marilyn Wilson-Hadid has experienced just how important communication is—both while sailing, and while on the job. And as she relates in the story that follows, she has seen the difference that good communication can make.

Says Wilson-Hadid, "During the same week, I raced aboard one boat that wasn't very competitive and one that was. One of the key differences that I noticed was the continual dialogue that was going back and forth between the captain and the crew on the competitive boat. The captain made it very clear what his intentions were in terms of his direction, but there were continual adjustments and input provided by the bowman—the guy on the front line. It was just like in business where the communication went from the president to marketing to sales to marketing to the president—it kept going back and forth.

"The team that communicated did so much better than the crew that was just sitting there, watching what was going on—knowing full well things were changing—but who weren't communicating back to the captain. If you are at the helm of a business, you have got to continually let people know when things are changing because market conditions change, competitive issues change, corporate challenges change, and so forth. And the most important communication isn't necessarily just from the helmsman speaking out, but the communication from the rest of the crew back to the helmsman."

ConvergeNet president and CEO Dick Watts finds that talking to employees is a great way to find out what they are all about—what their real interests and skills are. This is critical to getting the best efforts out of people. "Getting the best out of the resources that I'm given is something I spend a lot of time working on in both environments, both sailing and business. It means talking to people and understanding their skills and their needs as well. They're more likely to be better at the things they enjoy doing and they will make a bigger effort to improve if they're given an assignment that lines up with their desires. In some cases they might want to do something they've not done before. There's no such thing as a perfect organization in a company or on the water, and you really have to work with what you've got in the way of strengths and weaknesses. Understanding that in people— and talking with them about it—is a tremendous success factor in both environments."

When TechTouch Systems Doug Stewart conducts team-work training for businesspeople using sailboats, he is most concerned with getting the members of the team to build trust with one another by communicating openly and working closely together to achieve common goals. Says Stewart, "What we look at in terms of team building is, how do people support each other? How do you build the trust level? That's the key. The trust level has to be high for a team to be effective. And so a lot of the things we talk about are how you build trust. How do you do communications? How do you deal with issues? What do you do in crisis situations? What are your contingency plans? All of those things build trust.

"On the first night of the Caribbean Challenge, a few of us were sleeping in the aft bunks, where the deck is about two feet from your head. So two of the guys decided to go ashore and have a drink. Well, they came back about two in the morning having found friends to talk with, and began stomping around on the deck, just two feet over my head. I thought to myself, this is going to be a very long week unless we address this early. So the next morning over breakfast I said, 'Guys, there's something I've got to talk to you about. This is what happened, this is how I felt about it,' and so on. And they were very apologetic. They hadn't realized and said, 'Okay, we'll make sure that doesn't happen again.'

"Of course, I was happy that I wasn't going to get disturbed again at two in the morning, but more important, what that did was open up the possibilities for communication. So, when we were giving some instruction later in the day, one of the other crew members said, 'You know, it really works better for me if you talk to me in this fashion rather than in the fashion you're talking to me.' We had established enough trust early on to deal with truly tough issues when they came up. And that helped make that team what it was."

Involve Everyone and Delegate Authority

No matter how talented or smart or hardworking a manager might be, it's physically impossible for him or her to do every single thing to make a fair-sized business run. He can't answer every phone call, or schedule every appointment, or take part in every sales call, or machine every part. The very nature of being a manager is to accomplish work through others. So one of the most important skills for any manager is learning how to delegate responsibility *and* authority to the employees who need it to do their jobs effectively.

And delegation offers an added benefit—managers who delegate tasks to their employees get them more involved in the organization and in their work. Not only does this tend to result in better services and products—and happier customers—but it also tends to result in happier employees. And happier employees are a good thing for any business to have.

Pete du Pont, editor of *IntellectualCapital.com*, knows the power of delegating authority, and of involving his employees and crew in the work that they do. Says Du Pont, "We motivate our in-house staff—the people who write and produce our magazine—by pointing out that this is one of the first Internet magazines to come along in the public policy area and that they're pioneers. They're engaged in something exciting and we expect them to talk to us about what they think is good and bad about the stories and what the stories ought to be on.

"Similarly, when you're sailing—and it's even tougher if your crew is a bunch of volunteers, which in my experience virtually everybody is—you motivate people by making them an involved part of the crew and not a bunch of B-maxes who are supposed to just hold down the rail and keep their mouth shut.

"You have what I would call an open ship. You want feedback. You don't want a lot of yelling all at once, but you have to encourage organized communication. You tell one guy to watch for the waves and somebody else to keep an eye on the competitors—particularly that blue boat over there that seems to be particularly fast. You pick somebody else to think ahead about laylines (navigation). If you give everybody a task—preferably a task in addition to the primary job they're doing, whether it's as a trimmer or pit man or doing the bow—that keeps them involved and interested and ensures a flow of information back to you."

At Thomson Industries, John Thomson is also aware of the power of involving people in their jobs. Says Thomson, "Involve people. Let them know where you are and what's going on, and try to make them a part of the decision-making process. Ask them for their input, whether you agree with them or not—at least they will feel they have the venue to express their feelings, that they're part of the team. I've found that to be tremendously helpful."

Malin Burnham of John Burnham & Company goes so far as to say that delegation is the key to teamwork—one cannot exist without the other. Says Burnham, "To me, delegating authority equals teamwork. You can't just give somebody responsibility, you have to give them the authority within certain parameters to execute and to do without asking permission. So many people in business give their employees responsibility—'Okay, you're in charge of this area'—but they don't give them the authority to execute it. In sailing, if you're a trimmer, or a navigator, or whatever position you fulfill on the team, you've got to make decisions *and* you've got to call those shots. If, for example, you're the navigator, you can't just be responsible for telling somebody where we *are*—you've got to say where we're *going*."

Of course, it's a lot easier to talk about involving employees than it is to make it happen. Not only that, but delegating authority and involving employees is a full-time job. According to Tom Whidden, "It's a lot like what we do in sailing. We push the accountability down as far into the ranks as we can. You do that by including people in your vision, in your goals, in what you're trying to accomplish. You let the people share in the measuring of results so they can see how they're doing. Why? Because people like to achieve.

"In our company, we have a term, CNC, 'cost of non-conformance,' and we actually measure nonconformance. At our sailmaking sites, for example, everybody—including the people that sew sails—know the goals and know the numbers we're trying to achieve. They know what is consistent with profitability and what isn't. And they know if they make a mistake, or they don't conform, that it hurts the company and ultimately hurts them. That's how you get them to be accountable for what they do."

Dick Watts, president and CEO of ConvergeNet Technologies, feels that the best teamwork comes from shared responsibility. "If you can't get everybody involved to feel a part of the team and feel some vested interest in making it win, then the thing starts to fall apart in a hurry. But teamwork doesn't necessarily mean that everyone gets a vote on every decision or even gets to participate in every decision. In fact, far from it. One of the fundamentals of teamwork is everybody knows their place. It starts with an understanding of each individual's role so that everybody knows where they should be and when they are stepping out of that box.

"Where it can really fall down very hard is if nobody's sure about their role: 'Am I involved in this decision because it really is my job and they're helping me, or it's their job and I'm helping them?' It starts with people being comfortable that their assignment is clear—knowing that they're relatively comfortable and competent in it—and *then* participating as part of a team to reach a higher goal."

Treat Your People Right

As employees—and as human beings—we all want to be treated with respect and dignity, and we all want to feel that we are valued and appreciated for our contributions to the organizations we work for. However, we all know employees who are mistreated and abused, and bosses who think of little more than the bottom line. Sure, the bottom line is important—a healthy one helps to ensure the viability of the business—but there is no bottom line without the concerted effort of a team of employees dedicated to providing their very best efforts day in and day out.

According to J-Class Management's Elizabeth Meyer, "If you don't handle your people right, it infects all of them. If you are unfairly critical of a single employee, it will freak everybody out. No single thing is more important than handling the personnel issues. And that's true in sailboat racing, too. If you don't figure out the strongest suit of each one of your crew members, put them where they're strong, tell them exactly what you want them to do, and explain exactly how the communication system is going to work, you can't do anything. You can't just throw them all on deck and say, 'You figure it out.' You have to be very sensitive to who they are. And the more experienced they are, the more sensitive you have to be—especially if they've got big egos.

"For instance, right now I manage *Endeavour* and *Shamrock V*. There's nine crew on each boat and I have to deal with everything from people's family and financial problems, to ego problems, to little cat fights between them, to health problems. It's a major handholding job."

Treating people right means treating your employees the same way you would like to be treated yourself. And it means treating people in a way that encourages them to work toward your organization's goals and in accordance with its values. So, if you want people to take initiative and to be accountable for what they do on the job, you've got to encourage them to do just that—not punish them for it.

Tom Whidden encourages his employees to take initiative through his words and actions. "I want to show them that it's not bad to make a decision and be wrong—it's worse to make no decision at all. When a new employee doesn't work out, I'll say to the person who hired him, 'Look, you gave it a try—you used your best judgment to hire this person. You can't control who or what a person is, so why get down on yourself for making a mistake like that?' "

It's taken Pete du Pont a little while to learn this lesson, but learn it he has. "I think it comes with age. My wife will tell you that over the years I've learned to yell a lot less on the boat. She's said, 'When we first started racing after we were married and something would go wrong around the weather mark, you'd be screaming at the crew and directing people to do this and that. Meanwhile you'd be steering the boat all over the place. It was high, it was low, and nobody was trimming the mainsail because they were listening to you yell about the spinnaker. These days you don't.' "

"One thing I've learned is that people are going to straighten out the problem—that if I keep a little calmer, stay on my course, and do what I'm supposed to be doing it's much better than throwing winch handles. I once sailed with a Norwegian—a guy named Magnus Konow, who was an Olympic gold medalist in the 6 Meter class before World War II—who literally threw winch handles at the crew. If you did something wrong, he would scream at you in Norwegian and a winch handle would come flying forward. That style doesn't work anymore—in sailboat racing *or* in business."

The term "Captain Bligh" is often applied to the screamers on a sailboat. And they usually find it hard to keep a crew, because *no* one likes to be yelled at. Ted Turner has been known to raise his voice more than once in the heat of battle, but somehow he does it in a way that is not belittling to the crew, but rather serves as motivation—because it shows how much he wants to win. Once, during a match race regatta in Miami, Ted was concerned because the sails were not being pulled in quickly enough by his longtime teammate Bunky Helfrich. Needless to say, Ted did not keep this concern to himself. His tirade—in a raised voice— went something like this:

"Trim the sail, Bunky—Trim—Trim it now!!! **#&%$! I love you, Bunky, but just triiiiiiiiiim!!!!"*

Recognize and Reward

Most managers know the value of rewarding and recognizing the effort of their employees. The simple fact is, employees who are rewarded for doing a good job perform better, they provide better customer service, and they are happier and more satisfied with their jobs. Nevertheless, precious few managers actually put this knowledge into action.

In an elaborate eight-hundred-store study of the effect of employee attitudes recently conducted by Sears Roebuck, researchers found that there is a direct correlation between employee satisfaction and profitability. At Sears, if an employee's attitude on ten essential factors—including workload, treatment by bosses, and so forth—increases by 5 percent, then customer satisfaction will jump 1.3 percent, leading to a one-half-percentage-point rise in revenue. For Sears—with annual revenues of approximately $41 billion—this increase amounts to more than $200 million in additional revenues for the company per year.

According to Malin Burnham, chairman of John Burnham & Company, "You have to share the spoils with people. In sailing, that means you share the credits for winning. In the Star class, which is where I got started, there are two people on board—the skipper and the crew. We *always* had equal trophies for the skipper and the crew. One wasn't bigger and one smaller—they were equal. And if you win the Star Class World Championships, you were *both* world champions.

"In this business, we share profits, commissions, whatever it is. In other words, a producer in our business doesn't have to be a boss, he doesn't have to be an owner, but he shares in the profits of his productivity. I would say that just about every year over the last thirty years, one or more producers has made more money than has the president of the company."

DynaYacht's Chuck Robinson agrees that rewarding employees is a key way to make them even better and more effective team players. "I want people that have the feeling that they're sharing the enthusiasm, the excitement, the sense of creating. I want them to feel that they're creating with me, that it's not me creating and them doing their job.

"I've given stock to those who've been working with me and I continue to expand the concept of sharing whatever comes out of this effort. I've reached the point where what I make out of any of these ventures isn't going to change my lifestyle one way or another, so it isn't important to me. What *is* important is this sense of having created something and if we can do it as a team, I'll get the satisfaction I need to keep me going."

Chris Ericksen

Sales Manager, Allied Pacific Metal Stamping, Anaheim, California

"I recently was out of work and casting around for something to tell potential employers about myself, especially about my team-player ethos. In the middle of an interview, it came to me: I race sailboats! I told these folks that, as a kid, I was no kind of an athlete: too skinny for football, too short for basketball, no hand-eye coordination for baseball and I didn't swim well enough for water polo. But in racing sailboats I found the essence of teamwork: how the combined efforts of a team lead to success.

"I went on to say that, on my Etchells, I steer—but the best sailor on the boat is my partner, the tactician and sail trimmer: I steer because that is what I do best on that particular team. On the forty-footer I've sailed, I run the middle of the boat: before sets, jibes or whatever, I make sure everyone on the team knows their job and is ready and then I tell the helmsman. The pleasure of snapping off a perfect dippole jibe in twenty-two knots of wind is a great rush for me, because it means all nine of us did what we were supposed to do when we were supposed to do it—and I was part of it.

"I finished up by saying, I don't say where the Etchells is supposed to go, I just get it there. And on the forty-footer, I'm just the cheerleader. I don't need to be standing on the bow of the boat when we cross the finish line so that I cross the line first: the key is to cross the line as part of the winning team.

"I'm convinced that my deep appreciation for teamwork helped me land my current job: sales manager for a metal-stamping house. I don't design the tooling, or stamp the parts: all I do is invite people to buy parts from us. When I sell, I'm selling the team's efforts, not my own. And it is this aspect of winning—not by individual effort, but through teamwork that I carry from sailboat racing into the workplace."

Chapter Five

Rule Three —
Stack the Deck in Your Favor

The Transpac Race—Los Angeles to Honolulu—will always be one of the great ocean races
of the world. Run every two years in early July,
the racetrack has some of the most consistent—
and fun—sailing conditions in the world. After
spending a couple of days bashing along on a
close reach—with the sails trimmed tight, cold
Pacific waves lashing the foredeck and rail
where the crew is sitting—there is a magical

change. The wind begins to shift so it's blowing from behind, the water begins to warm, and you know you are
on the edge of the famous northeast trade winds. Soon
the heavy headsails used for sailing against the wind can
be exchanged for the lighter weight spinnakers that propel a racing boat downwind.

My first Transpac will always be my most memorable. It
was aboard Morrie Kirk's Santa Cruz 50 *Hana Ho*. Designed by Mr. "fast is fun" Bill Lee, the SC 50 is a downwind sled—narrow and extremely lightweight—built with
one thing in mind: surfing downwind fast to Hawaii! There
were eight other Santa Cruz 50s in the race, and some of the
West Coast's most experienced sailors were on their crews.
This made our class by far and away the most competitive
of the nearly one hundred boats in the race.

Halfway through the race, the daily position report indi-
cated that we were in third place among the 50s, positioned
midway between the lead boat to the south and the second-
place boat to the north. By then, we were deep into trade
wind country with big puffy cumulus clouds—the kind you
picture in the postcards from Hawaii—blowing in from behind with eight- to ten-foot swells lined up perfectly with
the wind. Ideal surfing conditions. Driving the boat in the
daytime was a joy, but at night—when the wind picked up
from a comfortable fifteen to twenty knots, to thirty plus
during a passing squall—it took all the concentration you
could muster to keep the boat on track. The rides on the
waves were incredible. Like a surfer at Diamond Head, a
wave would come up from behind and lift up our stern.
Then, with the wind pressing into the sails, the boat would

take off downhill, spray flying off the hull like a high-speed powerboat. The speedo regularly topped twenty knots during these rides.

Three hundred miles out from the finish line in Honolulu, the boat that had taken the southern track fell back. We had more wind to the north and were in a neck-and-neck duel with our sister ship *Shandu*—but where was she? We had not seen another boat in seven days—not abnormal for a 2,200 mile race, where even a slight course difference puts the boats miles apart in a few hours. Then, in the middle of the night, as we ghosted along in relatively mild conditions, a red light appeared on the horizon off to our right. As it got closer we could just make out the dark outline of sails. A boat crossed within a couple of boat lengths behind us, sailing on the opposite jibe. It was *Shandu*. That moment set up the most memorable finish to a yacht race I have ever experienced.

Throughout the night and the next day, we worked the boat to its max—constantly trimming the sails to perfection, and steering to try and catch every passing wave. But *Shandu* was out of sight, she had taken a northerly course to try to get more wind. We were in a battle for first place, but we could not see our nemesis. We had only our imagination to keep ourselves motivated.

Meanwhile, the excitement on board grew as we made landfall to the Hawaiian Islands, the peak of the volcano Mauna Kea on the Big Island emerging out of the clouds still over a hundred miles away. Needless to say, like any navigator, I was mildly relieved to see the highest point in the island chain right where it should have been. I had been relying on the "magic" of a satellite navigation unit and cross checking with my sextant for nearly two thousand miles.

Daytime turned to night as we sailed toward the steep Molokai coast. As the breeze started to build, we performed the final maneuver of the race—a jibe to bring the wind over the right quarter off our stern and take a course directly for the finish line at Diamond Head. But where was *Shandu*? With twenty-five miles to go to the finish, she couldn't be too far away. Had she found an advantage in her move to the north? Was she several miles ahead, out of sight in the pitch-black moonless night?

All of a sudden, we saw her coming in from the north, her red and green bow lights dipping in and out of sight as she surfed the building waves. She approached until she was no more than a hundred yards away and then jibed, dead abeam, and now pointed at the finish line, too. It was a drag race. After nearly ten days of sailing, and 2,200 miles of Pacific Ocean, two sister ships were side by side headed to the finish. Wow!!

The body of water between the islands of Molokai and Oahu is called the Molokai Channel, and it is famous for its big winds and big waves. It's as if the entire Pacific is trying to funnel between the two islands. The waves build to truly enormous size, and the wind nearly doubles in intensity. Extreme conditions for a drag race to the finish.

I was at the helm, the on-deck stereo was blasting "Mountain Jam" by the Allman Brothers, and the crew was working the sails continuously. Out of the corner of my eye, I could see that *Shandu* was matching us wave for wave. But in the darkness something seemed strange: they were pumping their mainsail! Employing a technique developed for lightweight racing dinghies, their crew was rapidly pulling in the sail—like a fan—to try and propel the boat like a bird flapping its wings. It required the intense full-time effort of two crew to do the pumping. Seeing that, we started pumping our sail, too—something had to give.

At that moment, with dolphins jumping on either side of the bow—as if welcoming us to the islands—stars twinkling in the sky overhead, and the Pacific swells providing intense roller-coaster–like sleigh rides down their faces, I got in the zone. It was if I was sailing my Laser—a one-man dinghy—downwind; it was all about steering to perfection. Turn up to gain speed just before the wave lifts the transom, then, at just the right moment, point the bow straight downhill to begin the surf. Then turn ever so slightly to the right just before reaching the trough to try to extend the free ride for as long as possible. Ten waves, twenty, the crew was reporting gains.

After nearly an hour of driving, I was emotionally and physically exhausted. I had never tried so hard in all my life, and I was spent. I asked for relief and handed off the helm to one of our many ace helmsmen, Tom Willson, and looked behind. There was *Shandu*—a tenth of a mile astern—the margin a product of the hard work and concentration by everyone on board.

We crossed the famous finish line abeam of Diamond Head lighthouse nearly a minute and a half ahead of *Shandu*. First place in the Transpac Race with a finish like that, it just does not get any better! After the traditional 4 A.M. welcoming parties—replete with flowered leis and Mai-tai punch—it was off to bed, for the longest sleep any of us had had in nearly two weeks. Hey, nobody said sailboat racing was easy!

Competition, the drive to win—to put forth every asset or advantage, every ounce of strength and determination that you can summon out of yourself, or out of your organization—is paramount to success. For many of our group, the love of competition is what makes sailboat racing—and business—interesting and fun.

And both sailboat racing and business have a long history of doing whatever it takes to stack the deck in your favor. In sailboat racing, boat speed is everything. This means building boats that are lighter, possessing sleeker, more slippery hulls, more aerodynamic sails. Boats that can turn on a dime and hold up in rough conditions. And then it means recruiting the most talented crew you can find. In the same way, in business today, being fast and flexible are everything. This means building organizations that are light and agile, that are wired together with the best and latest computing and telecommunications technology, that can change direction at a moment's notice, and then recruiting the most talented employees you can find.

In sailboat racing there is a saying that "boat speed is king," and it is very true. In formula classes like those that race in the America's Cup and the Volvo Ocean Race, teams and their designers spend countless hours looking for an edge, and the result are boats that measure in within the formula (like an Indy car or Formula One) but are all slightly different—different hulls, keels, and rudders and sail plans (although they may all look the same to an unpracticed eye). An America's Cup design team might spend upward of 33 percent of a team's entire budget trying to get an edge in boat speed—it's that important. In 1992, Bill Koch's *America³* campaign utilized four America's Cup boats during a multiyear testing program that would rival a NASA space effort, to develop *USA-23*—the boat that ultimately was entered in and won the America's Cup.

But even in the strict one-design classes where the boats must measure within very strict tolerances, a boat speed edge is possible and strived for. It's amazing what a small difference in speed it takes to enjoy a huge advantage when racing in a big fleet. In a short buoy race of one hour in length, if you can get to the first mark just a couple of boat lengths faster than the competition, that could well be enough to assure victory.

But let's be clear right now. Stacking the deck in your favor does not mean cheating. Although cheating does occur in sailboat racing—as in any sport—*real* champions play by the rules. They are smart enough and cunning enough to gain an advantage within the rules. I have raced with the likes of Dennis Conner, Ted Turner, and Dave Ullman and I have never seen any of them ever break a rule. Rather they are often the first to do a penalty turn if they foul, and they *always* make sure they know the rules of the race before the starting gun sounds.

Stacking the deck means using every tool at your disposal to give your organization an advantage in the marketplace: the best people, the latest technology, the deepest commitment, the most resources, and so forth, but all within the rules or laws. Sailboat racing is, for the most part, self-policing. It is steeped in what is known as the Corinthian tradition—this is the foundation of the sport, an assumption that competitors will play fairly, by the rules.

Protect Your Competitive Advantage

The ideal situation in business is to have a competitive advantage over the competition. Your competitive advantage can be in almost any area of your business—from lower costs of production, to better, more advanced technology, to a deeper line of credit, to happier, more productive employees. The key to success in the long run, however, is not just to have a competitive advantage, but to maintain it over a long period of time, and to create new competitive advantages in other areas of your business.

In some cases, just being the first to market with a new idea or the first company to move business in a certain direction provides a significant competitive advantage. Unless the idea is patentable or somehow able to be kept secret from your competitors (like the *very* closely guarded formula for Coca-Cola), however, then chances are, the advantage won't last for very long.

The best way to protect your competitive advantage is to keep moving, to keep improving year after year. A business that stands still is a business that is doomed.

According to United Technologies Corporation chairman and CEO George David, "You have to get better every year. These Grand Prix boats don't have long lives, it would be great if you could get four years. But even inside that period, you have to improve each year. Over the years, I've felt that the edge, or the improvement in handicap versus actual speed, needs to be in the range of three seconds a mile each year. You have to do new foils (the keel and rudder), or change the mast, or pad or bump the hull (to change its shape for optimal handicap). If you don't make changes that will get you this three seconds a mile, you're going to be 'out the back,' as we say on the racecourse.

"The same is true in business. You need five percent productivity gains each year in most businesses, or you're going to start to lose ground. But I think it's in each one of us to think that what we do today is the best that we can ever do. So we resist change, the notion that we can get better. Yet, the fact is that we can, experience shows this overwhelmingly and again and again. The best crews and the best business people step up to this all the time, they make gains happen, and that's how they stay on top.

"I've changed my mind on this gain thing, and dramatically over the last ten years. When I was younger at UTC, the name of the game was to set a low business plan, beat it, get a nice bonus, and have senior management say, 'Great job.' But there was an amazing shift in the way the best American companies were run about fifteen years ago, under the influence of the Japanese assault on many of our markets. The best of us learned in response, and often we learned from the Japanese. What we learned was the 'process revolution,' that is, to focus on and re-engineer all of our processes, rather than to focus just on engineering and product launch and marketing, which had been the priorities for most of corporate America for most of the postwar period. What we found when we went after process was that the productivity gains were astonishing. And the best companies and executives learned quickly to set really high targets and to expect to achieve them. The old ways were out the window. This has been the most profound change I have seen in my years in business, and the next ranked change isn't even close.

"What's different is that we have the confidence to set high goals, because experience has taught us that we can achieve them. If you don't have this confidence, you don't belong in the boardroom, or on the racecourse."

Know Your Environment

The person who is most familiar with his or her environment—whether it's the environment represented by your business markets, or the environment in which you race your sailboat—has a clear and often unbeatable advantage over those who aren't. Know your environment, and you'll prosper. Ignore it, and you'll soon find yourself far behind the rest of the pack.

According to Elizabeth Meyer of J-Class Management: "In sailing, you have to be very sensitive to current and wind and weather. Some people are naturally that way. I'm more somebody who learns it. I've got to study it and research what the conditions are going to be during the race. Then you've got to find who your competition is. There are some people in the fleet you can just ignore, because they're nowhere near as good as you are. And then there are some people in the fleet who are so good you can ignore them, too—just watch them go. I'm usually in the high middle of the fleet. Before a race, I figure out who my nemesis is, who

I'm racing against. Then I *really* concentrate on those people and make sure they don't get by me. And that's also a very important thing to do in business. If you have a business that has competition, identify who the competition is and really keep your eye on them. Cover them."

Manage by Self-Induced Crisis

Some of the world's greatest innovations, and some of its greatest businesses and organizations, are a product of crisis. The Internet—originally conceived as a way for military and government officials to communicate with one another during a war—exists because of the Cold War and the threat of nuclear Armageddon. Many of NASA's innovations—innovations that have found their way into many everyday commercial products today—came about as a direct result of the crisis atmosphere created by President Kennedy's goal for the United States to be the first to land a manned mission on the Moon. And the inexpensive, but extremely accurate GPS direction-finding systems that have found their way into cars, boats, and the hands of people all around the world owe their existence to a series of satellites that the U.S. military launched years ago to track the movements of troops and military equipment.

Chuck Robinson knows the power of crisis, and he has found out how to harness this power to accomplish great things. "When I was at business school at Stanford, I evolved the concept of management by self-induced crisis. All the progress in this world comes out of crisis. If there isn't a crisis, there's no tension—it's in the state of tension that you solve problems and you move forward. And you can either have somebody create those crises for you or you create your own. I decided that creating my own was a better way of doing it.

"And one other principle that has always been important to me is the competitive situation. Everybody says, 'Give me a level playing field to compete on.' I say, 'How stupid can you be?' The game is to tilt the playing field in your favor. You tilt the playing field by anticipating the flow of history and positioning yourself to take advantage of things that are going to develop on ahead. If you make a decision based on all the facts you know today, you're bound to be wrong because the gestation period for taking an idea to commercial exploitation can be one year or five years or even ten years. So if you make a decision based on what the conditions are today, you're bound to be wrong.

"You have to ask yourself, 'What are the factors that are bringing about change, and where is that going to lead three years from now, or five years from now? What do I need to do today to be positioned to advantage when this all comes together?' That's what I mean by inducing your own crises. And as soon as you make that decision, my God, you've got a bundle of crises out ahead dealing with the problems that decision generates. But as long as you have properly—with sensitivity—anticipated the flow of history, it's not the decision you made, but how you deal with the crises that it generates that determines whether you're going to be successful or not."

Of course, Chuck Robinson's theory flies in the face of all the things that we are taught in business school or on the job about putting a premium on preventing crises, or putting out the fires as soon as they erupt. Chuck tells about the time he lectured a group of business students about the way he does business. "The graduate school of business at the University of Southern California asked me, as the president of a major international mining and shipping company, to talk to their senior class and all of their faculty on my principles of management. I told the assembled group, 'You know, as long as you're sensitive to the flow of history, it doesn't much matter what the decision is. It's how you deal with the crisis that your decision generates that will determine whether you're successful.'

"Well, I heard a gasp. I had destroyed everything that the professors had talked about in terms of calculating risk and getting all your facts together and making decisions on a sound basis. They never invited me back because I destroyed two years of management and science that they had been taught by their professors. But you know what? I had an application from almost everyone in that class. They wanted to come and work for me."

Play by the Rules

In today's world of media- and advertiser-powered sports stars, the America's Cup—with its huge, seventy-five-foot-long, twenty-five-ton boats—or the globe-girdling Volvo Ocean Race—with its powerful sixty-five-foot sloops—are the general public's idea of the ultimate sailing competition. But inside the world of sailboat racing, most sailors will agree that the Olympic Games, raced in much smaller boats, is a more prestigious sailing event—the preeminent test of pure sailing skills. And if there were a vote to choose the ultimate Olympic sailboat class (of which there are nine), surely the Star boat would lead the fleet.

The Star is a true classic, a boat that was born in a much simpler time and place. Designed in 1911 by Francis Sweisguth, the Star is just twenty-two feet in length, and requires a crew of only two to sail. It has a towering mast and huge sail plan—even by today's standards—and for many in the world of sailing winning the Star Class World Championships means reaching the pinnacle of the sport.

The list of Star Class World Champions reads like a Who's Who of the best and the brightest in the world of sailing. Names like Dennis Conner, Buddy Melges, Tom Blackaller, Lowell North, Paul Cayard—all world champions in the fabled Star boat. And as the oldest sailboat still racing in the Olympics—introduced at the 1932 Los Angeles Games—the Star has a long and distinguished history.

In 1945—at age seventeen—Malin Burnham became the youngest sailor ever to win the Star Class World Championships. And while Malin has had a long and illustrious career in sailing since then—he was responsible for organizing Dennis Conner's successful 1987 America's Cup Challenge that brought the Cup home from Perth, Australia, to San Diego, and he has skippered or crewed in countless races—he still looks back fondly to his days racing Star boats.

While he savors his many victories, however, there is one story about a race Malin didn't win that speaks volumes about the kind of man he is, and about the kind of company that he runs.

It was at the 1963 Star Class World Championship on Lake Michigan, and here's how Burnham relates the story:

"After three races, we were seven points ahead of the fleet of fifty-some entries. Unlike today, where organizers anchor inflatable buoys to establish the course, the marks on that particular course were anchored Ensign sailboats, which are about twenty-four feet long. As we approached the first weather mark in the fourth race, we were in second place. We came in on a port layline with plenty of room— nobody pushing us. As we rounded the boat, the Ensign suddenly swung toward us. As a result, the mast and rigging of the Ensign and the last two feet of my sail hit. Nobody saw it except me. Without thinking twice, I immediately turned back to the harbor.

"Well, needless to say, everybody wondered why I was sailing for the dock. It was simple; I fouled and I was out of the race. We could've done ten laps around that boat and still won the world championship. Unfortunately, in those days there were no throw-out races. It was a five-race series, and if you had a bad race or you broke down or fouled out, that was it. You could just pack it up and go home. And there was no redress on fouls, including hitting a turning mark. So this little foul cost us the race—and the world championship. Everybody felt sorry for us when we got into the dock, but there wasn't anything that I or anyone else could do about it. I pulled our boat out and said, 'Well, it's my own damn fault—just carelessness. Don't feel sorry for us, we'll just go out and win tomorrow's race.' "

Malin could have easily won a second world championship at that regatta—he had the speed and was sailing better than any of the competition, but due a combination of bad luck and cutting the turning mark a little too close, he broke a rule of sailing. No one else saw the touch, and he could have kept sailing and won the Worlds. But Malin played the game by the rules and he is the better man as a result. He has won far more victories—both in business, and on the water—playing by the rules.

For Jack Woodhull, ethics are the foundation on which you build an organization. Without a firm moral compass, there literally is no company. "Ethics are *very* important, and we focused on this at Logicon. We never wanted to be accused of cheating or even being technically dishonest. At our periodic meetings with outside analysts, I was often asked why this was so important to me. I told them, 'If we don't have high ethical standards, then we won't have a business—it's as basic as that.' As a result of this focus, we built a great reputation within our industry.

"On a sailboat—in a race—ethics and honesty are just as important. Reputations matter, even in racing. If you foul another boat—as we did in a recent race—you do your penalty [in this case a 720-degree turn], and keep racing. We could have pretended that nothing happened and kept racing, and then gone into a protest hearing after the race and argued that we did not foul the other boat. It was very, very close, but *we* knew we had crossed the line, and you have to face up to what you did wrong. In that race, we immediately did our penalty turns and were pretty far behind, but we kept working hard and didn't give up. Ultimately, we sailed back up into the fleet and placed pretty well. Maybe the good Lord helped us!"

Jack Woodhull on Ethics

* Maintain the highest ethical standards
* Don't cut corners
* If you are in trouble, admit it
* Be honest and aboveboard in all your dealings
* Your word should be *golden*

Whether or not you believe that "what goes around comes around," it's clear that you can't expect others to be honest with you if you aren't first honest with them. And by taking the moral high ground, you set an example for others—an example that is unambiguous and deeply rooted in a desire to do what's right. Jack Woodhull continues, "Ethics set the tone for your organization and for your industry. If you have high ethical standards, then internal bickering goes down. So you see an effect, not only in the marketplace, or in the way your competitors treat you, but also within the organization—or on the crew of a boat."

Ben Mitchell on Jack Woodhull and Ethics

Ben Mitchell was Vice President-General Counsel of Logicon for eighteen years. He first met Jack while he was in college. It was at the prestigious Congressional Cup match racing regatta and Benny picked Jack's boat out of the hat to race aboard. They stayed in touch over the years and, when Benny finished law school, Jack came up to him in his matter-of-fact style and said, "You're working for me." He did. As Vice President-General Counsel of Logicon during the company's heyday and ultimate sale to Northrop, he has a solid perspective on the way Jack does business.

Says Mitchell, "Jack's ethical backbone is beyond reproach. Never would anybody be able to propose anything that wouldn't stand the light of day. And we had competitors that absolutely did not play by the same set of rules. For example, they had no misgivings about hiring a guy right out of the government that had been working on a particular program when he should have had a one-year exclusion. They would give him six months to bring that program in or he was out the door."

"I think one of the reasons we were ultimately rewarded over the long run was our ethics. Some of these other companies might have grown faster than we did because they had lesser standards. But during the period when ethical standards were not enforced as strongly as they are today, and influence pedaling was very prevalent in the business environment, we were just completely immune. We were above reproach because that was just not the way we played the game, and everyone in the business knew it. So as a result we grew more slowly during this period, but very, very profitably.

"On the racecourse, Jack is the same way, we play strictly by the rules and everyone knows it. He is so ethically strong—it is really admirable."

Sailing Terms and Their Business Corollaries

Douglas Stewart, CEO of TechTouch Systems of Santa Fe, New Mexico, has seen the positive impact that sailboat racing can have on businesspeople, and he has found that the effects can be dramatic, and lasting.

Here is Doug Stewart's list of common sailing terms and definitions—and their business corollaries—borrowed from his highly successful SailRite leadership and team-building program for businesspeople using sailboat racing as the classroom:

Blanketing	*def—Using your sails to block the wind of your competitor.* A business strategy that reduces competitor effectiveness.
Broad reach	*def—A fast and easy point of sail with the wind coming from behind the boat.* The most efficient phase of performance.
Close hauled	*def—Sailing as close to the wind as possible.* Moving the business as close to the visioned direction as possible.
Gust	*def—A sudden puff of wind.* Sudden outside force that requires immediate action.
Heeling	*def—Tipping of the boat caused by wind blowing on the sails.* A situation that causes concern until the organization learns how to control it.

In irons	*def—An undesirable condition when the boat remains pointed directly towards the wind until all forward motion stops.* Brought to a standstill by market factors; requires a change to get underway again.
Jibe	*def—Turning the boat so the wind causes the sail to blow across rapidly to the other side.* Dramatic change of direction, inflicting great stress on team or business if done incorrectly.
Leeway	*def—Sideslipping—an undesirable condition when the sails are trimmed incorrectly.* Organization slipping laterally away from desired destination/direction.
Luffing	*def—Flapping of the sails caused by incorrect sail trim.* A situation in which maximum effectiveness is not being made of available resources.
Luffing up	*def—An aggressive maneuver intended to cause a competitor to change course.* An aggressive, legal maneuver to keep a competitor from passing.
Pinching	*def—Steering too close to the wind for optimal performance.* Setting the course too aggressively—loses speed.

Planing/surfing	*def—Sailing's version of "warp speed" caused by favorable winds and big waves pushing the boat forward.* Exceeding nominal performance limits through exceptional planning and teamwork.
Tacking	*def—Changing direction so the wind blows on the opposite side of the boat and sails.* Changing organizational direction to reach goals/vision.
Telltales	*def—Yarn or ribbon taped to the sails indicating the direction of the air flow and aiding efficient sail trim.* Indicators of directional flow: customer service, market share, morale, et al.
True wind	*def—The wind direction felt by a sailboat at rest as opposed to "apparent wind" which is felt when the boat is moving.* The true state of the organization relative to the market or business climate.

Chapter Six

Rule Four —
Be Prepared to Change
Course Quickly

One of my most memorable sailing experiences was aboard a boat that was designed and built over a decade before World War II—a floating antique. But at 134 feet long, the J-boat *Endeavour* looks like anything but an antique. She is, in my mind, the most beautiful sailboat in the world. So a few years ago when Elizabeth Meyer's office called to see if I would be interested in coming out to Newport, Rhode Island, to sail on *Endeavour*, I jumped at the chance.

The occasion was the arrival of *Endeavour* in the United States. My friend Gary Jobson, ESPN's sailing guru, had convinced Elizabeth to stage a match race—to turn back the clocks to the golden era of yachting—between *Endeavour* and another J-boat, Sir Thomas Lipton's *Shamrock V*. Nothing like this had happened in Newport since the final America's Cup before World War II in 1937.

The plan was for Gary to steer one boat and Ted Turner the other. I got to be Ted's tactician and help him organize a crew of over thirty sailors. The crew included some of the most experienced big-boat crew in America, but not one of us had ever sailed on anything even close in size to *Endeavour*. The sheer scale and magnitude of the boat was incredible. Even the smallest sail bag took a host of crew members to lift. To give you an idea of the size of a J-boat's mast, there were only three bridges in America at the time that the boats could fit under.

So, with one afternoon practice under our belts, we headed out to Narragansett Bay to sail a match race between two J-boats. The spectator fleet was larger than anything I had ever seen in any America's Cup. Everyone wanted to witness the spectacle close up. We circled each other before the start, had a tacking duel going to weather, and set the enormous spinnaker at the top mark. But everything seemed to be happening in slow motion. No maneuver could even begin until the thirty-odd team members were all informed of the action—and prepared in their respective positions—no matter how much Ted or I willed it to happen faster. Once we got the boat up to full speed, you could sense the power as the hull thrust aside huge amounts of water. But looking at the speedometer, there was nothing incredible about the boat speed, in fact it was downright mediocre. For all their power, size, and glory these J-boats were nothing special when it came to performance.

In a race against today's fleet of hi-tech racing machines, that lack of maneuverability and only average speed would relegate these glorious J's to the back of the fleet, but nothing compares to their beauty and majesty! Plus with all the amenities of home down below (there are even heated towel racks in the bathroom), who needs to race these boats—let's go cruising!

Decades ago, people put a premium on businesses that didn't change—that could be counted on to be the same this year as they were last year, and the year before that, and the year before that. We felt very secure giving our phone business to good old Ma Bell. If our companies bought computers (in those days, room-sized mainframes), then IBM made us feel all warm and fuzzy inside. And the largest corporation of them all—General Motors—sold more cars to us than any other manufacturer. Each of these large companies had carved out its piece of the pie, and the pace of change was slow and steady.

That was then, and this is now.

Be Decisive

Ask any manager what he or she does best, and it's likely you'll hear this answer: make decisions. And it's true. The typical day for the typical manager is chock-full of decisions.

That's because the primary job of a manager is to allocate resources—both human and financial. And for most managers, the balancing of resources—and the issues, opportunities, and problems that arise in the natural course of business—lead to an ongoing need to make decisions.

Who will work overtime this weekend? How much money should I set aside in my rework budget for the quarter? Should we staff our vacancy with a temp or with a permanent employee? What can I do to reduce our turnover problem and improve the quality of our recruits? If you're not making decisions, either you're not a manager, or you're dead.

The ability to make decisions quickly and with confidence is very high on former Logicon, Inc., chairman Jack Woodhull's list of key business skills. Says Woodhull, "In a sailboat race, if you're not decisive about what you're going to do, and if you don't stick to your plan, you're going to get into an awful lot of trouble. And that's definitely true in business as well. In business if you're wishy-washy, you end up with people going off in different directions. Then they get upset when nobody knows what's going on, what they're all about, and what they're willing to do and not do."

In sailing, the best tacticians have all learned the importance of being decisive—even when they realize their decisions still have some degree of risk. One of the worst things a tactician can do is to display indecision to the crew. They want the tactician to provide a clear direction to go. So over the years, I have learned to internalize my decision-making process. While my brain may be asking, "Left or right?" or "Tack or stay the course?" I make a point of not appearing indecisive to the crew. That doesn't mean I forgo input from the team, but I try to give this tactical process the appearance of a very positive procedure with a definite end in sight! The results for team morale can be amazing. It may simply be human nature, but a crew member likes a decisive tactician—even if his or her batting average is a little lower than the guy who wears the decision-making process on his sleeve.

Sometimes decisions in a sailboat race have to be made right *now* to take advantage of an opportunity such as a wind shift or a competitor's mistake, or to recover from a setback like a crew error. Similarly, as the speed of business and technological change increase, decision-making in business is becoming more rapid—and the impact of not doing so can have severe consequences.

According to Malin Burnham, "Decision-making on the racecourse often has to be done in single-digit seconds. Other times you have a little bit more time to plan ahead. I suppose if you're sailing around the world, there are times you've got a couple of days to make a decision. But if you're sailing in a buoy race, with a buoy to round every few minutes, sometimes you literally don't have ten seconds to make a decision.

"Sometimes, and this applies in both yacht racing and in business, decisions are made prematurely and you move backward instead of forward. Other times they're made too late, and the result is the same. When you make a decision in life—whether it's sailing or business—and it's the *wrong* decision, the best thing you can do is undo it. Unfortunately, many people don't have the ability (or the intestinal fortitude) to undo wrong decisions or to change their mind. Sometimes—in the middle of a sailboat race or the middle of a business negotiation—you have to bail out and take a small loss to keep on track in the big picture."

And contrary to the popular opinion that it's always better to make a decision—any decision—than to make no decision at all, Malin begs to differ. "There's got to be a strategic or tactical reason for making a decision—both in sailing and in business. It isn't a matter of, 'Well, we've got to make a decision sooner or later.' "

According to Fisher-Price's Marilyn Wilson-Hadid, good decision-making is critical to a company's ability to capitalize on opportunities. "Many companies miss lots of opportunities because they can't make the call. They prefer to let the competition tell them the way to go. By definition, this puts you in second place."

Drew Freides, another accomplished sailor and yacht designer, who is currently working on his MBA at the Darden Graduate School of Business Administration at the University of Virginia, believes that once you have enough information to make an intelligent decision, then you should do just that. Freides says, "I've learned from sailing that it's often best not to wait for all the information before you make a decision because if you wait too long to make it, you're going to miss the opportunity. It's a matter of realizing that the information you've got at hand is sufficient and you should make a decision now rather than wait for every last detail to come clear. You're going to be right some of the time, and wrong in others, but at least you took advantage of the opportunity."

According to DynaYacht's Chuck Robinson, one of the worst things you can do when making a decision is to over-analyze the situation. Says Robinson, "There's a tendency to overanalyze and overcalculate—to try to get everything before making a decision. When I joined the board of the management consulting firm Arthur D. Little, and attended my first board meeting, I was told that its greatest asset was that twelve hundred employees had doctorate degrees. At that time, the company was making about three or four million dollars a year in profit. And I said, 'You know, there's something very strange to me about this. You have twelve hundred people who have their doctorates and you're making three to four million dollars a year profit. My company makes fifty to one hundred million dollars a year profit and I don't have one doctorate in my entire organization!'

"My point was that, you can have all the intellectual horsepower in the world, but if you don't direct it with imagination and a willingness to take chances and be creative, it doesn't add up to very much. Here's an example of what I like to see. I had one fellow who had graduated from the Stanford Business School working for me for about six or seven years. At that time, I was looking for someone to handle my marketing and he seemed the natural choice, but I eventually selected a fellow with an engineering background and appointed him vice president in charge of marketing.

"The fellow who had been with me longer came to me and said, 'You know, I'm just terribly shattered by your decision. I've worked for you for many years and I think you would have to admit that I have never made a mistake.' And I said, 'That's the problem. If you've never made a mistake, then you've never made a decision on time. If you were one hundred percent certain you're right, then you're too late. I want somebody who will be right eighty or ninety percent of the time, but who is prepared to fail. You're *never* prepared to fail and, as a result, you're not moving us forward.' He stopped and thought about it, and said, 'I guess I'll go out and fail at something.' I said, 'Well, you just failed at making vice president. Why don't you think about it?' "

Three-time America's Cup winner—and president of North Marine Group—Tom Whidden says that even if you make the wrong decision, you've got to bounce right back and keep making decisions. "There's only one American tactician that's ever lost the America's Cup—and he did it twice—that's me. But I've also won it three times. There's a lesson there for business. I could have said, 'Hey, I won one and I lost one. Why don't I just retire now?' But my decision was immediate—to try to win it back." And win it back he did—with Dennis Conner and the rest of the *Stars & Stripes* crew in 1987.

A Sailor's Guide to Investing

By Dean Brenner, Investment Executive, PaineWebber, Inc., Hartford, Connecticut

When I compare and contrast the two-part harmony of my life—pursuit of an Olympic medal in sailing, and my career as an investment manager at PaineWebber—many common threads appear. Success on the racecourse and managing your clients' portfolios share several characteristics. However, the common denominator between being a world-class sailor and a successful money manager lies within one word: *perspective*. One must have the *perspective* to keep one eye firmly on the big picture; the *perspective* to avoid taking excessive risk, the *perspective* to understand your strengths and to work within them; the *perspective* to keep your goals in mind and to work toward achieving them over the long term; and the *perspective* to maximize your role within your team, and make yourself and everyone around you better.

1. **The successful sailor outlines realistic goals and a strategy prior to entering the regatta.** From your goals will evolve your strategy. Will we sail this regatta looking to hit a home run on each leg, or will we try to hit singles all week? So too with investing. If your goal is to consistently beat the S&P 500 index by two percentage points each year, then you are being unrealistic and setting yourself up for failure. Set realistic goals, on the racecourse and in your portfolio, and you will increase your chances of success.

2. **The successful sailor has the patience to remain true to the strategy during periods of difficulty.** Generally speaking, if you choose the wrong side of the racecourse, you can still be successful if you work hard to win your side of the racecourse. Trust your instincts and remain true to your strategy. In investing, there will always be companies whose stock is performing well, and you won't catch them all. Remain faithful to what you know, and the companies and industries you have committed to.

3. **The successful sailor has the perspective to see the big picture.** When I am racing, approaching another boat on the other tack, I ask myself, *Do I want to keep*

going or should I tack and go the other way? Which side is winning, and is the difference significant enough for me to completely alter my pregame strategy? The prudent investor is continually asking himself, *Where can I get the best return on my investment, and still meet my financial goals?* Always keep your eye on the big picture.

4. **The successful sailor has the conviction to make decisions during tough times.** You are on the last leg of the race, and you have placed your boat on the wrong side of the racecourse the entire race. You have not made a correct decision all day. How do you react? The successful sailor, and the successful investor, maintains the self-confidence to continue trusting his or her instincts and making decisions. Always have an opinion, and always be decisive.

Be Nimble

Several years ago, Rosabeth Moss Kanter—Harvard Business School professor and one of the world's preeminent management gurus—wrote a book entitled *When Giants Learn to Dance*. When she wrote her book, the nation's largest corporations were just waking up to a fact that small, entrepreneurial start-ups had known for some time—that an ability to change course quickly was an essential element for prospering in today's fast and furious, technology-driven economy.

Mike Spence, former dean of the Stanford Graduate

School of Business, and an avid sailboarder, has seen the effect of today's business environment on organizations first-hand. "You don't have complete control over the environment—it's constantly changing, so you keep having to adapt to it and planning to adapt to it."

America's Cup winner and Oxbow Corporation founder and president Bill Koch has found great success—both in sailing and in business. According to Koch, "You've got to make sure the changes are real before you try to change, or readjust your whole organization, but on the other hand, the reverse is true as well. If the wind is shifting all over the place, you've got to maneuver constantly to take advantage of the shifting winds—you can't plan on one brute course and expect to win. The biggest lesson for my business is that we've got to change and we've got to be flexible.

"And if you have a mishap, you've got to recover from it. You know there's an old saying in sailing, if you've got into a hole you've got to get out of it quickly. In my business, we've had tremendously shifting conditions in the last three years with the deregulation of the power business. Before, we were fat, and had big fat healthy profitable contracts. When those disappeared, we had to get out in the marketplace and adapt to conditions that changed daily, whereas before they hadn't changed for ten years.

"We've got a coal mine in Colorado that mines four million tons of coal a year. Earlier this year, we had a mine fire followed by an explosion. Fortunately, no one was killed. We said, 'Guys, we've got to recover from this.' It's like breaking your spinnaker pole during a race. You've got to recover very quickly, you've got to still stay in the race, *and* you've got to fix it. And our guys were very good because when we had to shut the mine down, they went out and bought coal from others to supply all of our customers and keep our contracts in place. And then they methodically went about the processes of putting the fire out and decontaminating the mine. They started back up again about twice as fast as people expected them to. For them, it was all a matter of asking 'What's our long-term goal, how are we going to achieve it, and how flexible can we be in these changing circumstances?' "

John Bertrand, vice chairman of Quokka Sports, has been through disasters of his own, but he has been able to turn them around, recover quickly, and get back into the fight. One of the worst was a moment that millions have seen on television, when his boat, *oneAustralia*, broke and sunk while sailing against Team New Zealand's boat *Black Magic* in the 1995 America's Cup Challenger trials. "The boat broke up and sank really fast—in like two and a half minutes. We never really went through the 'what-if-the-boat-broke' scenario beforehand—it was something beyond any sailor's expectation. You think about what to do if the mast breaks. You know what you're going to do if you lose someone overboard. If someone is killed on the boat, you understand what's going to happen. But we never actually went through the what-ifs if the boat broke in two and sank.

"That was a management issue internally which, as chairman of the organization, I take full responsibility for. When you look at the America's Cup effort, there are three major links in the chain that holds the program together. If any of those links weaken, the whole thing falls apart. First, there's technology—it generally relates to boat speed, and it's got to be absolutely world-class. If it's not, well then the team dies in the process. The second element is organization—the administration including fund-raising. No cash, no splash, as they say. And then the third element is people, and that's probably the biggest untapped resource that we know.

"And this all relates to business, too. Technology, of course, is fundamental for the modern-day business. Organization is critical—quality control, finance control, critical path planning, corporate fulfillment, and marketing. And, finally, there are the people, that key final link. When you're putting these teams of people together, these organizations—whether you've got a team of twenty people, or you've got a team of two thousand people—the challenge is how do you get these people to really work with each other? And then you have the glue within—the cultural values, the integrity of the organization, the communication, the humor, and the focus—all of these wonderful elements that are very, very important for any successful business, and generally are missing or flawed for unsuccessful businesses or teams.

"So with our *oneAustralia* effort, in hindsight there were some technical areas that we didn't look at critically enough. We were running at too fine a safety margin and we didn't know it. It was an internal management issue and we paid the consequences which were pretty dramatic—the first team to ever sink a boat in the America's Cup competition!

"When it went down, there was not a trace left except one spinnaker pole that shot out of the water like an Exocet missile, and one totally cocooned spinnaker that popped out. There was nothing else, just bubbles and a memory. I remember the wind vane, which is on top of the mast, disappearing at about thirty miles an hour headed straight down and that was it—unbelievable.

"And then the issue was, okay, what do we do now? War experience shows that when people are under real pressure, they can operate effectively only when they're given a finite number of objectives to follow. More than three and people can't handle it in a life-and-death situation—their brains start to fuzz. So, we immediately embarked on a very, very, very clear, concise, and simple step-by-step process of rebuilding our first-generation pace boat. Just going through that step-by-step process was important to the team. Also, there was no blaming people—there's plenty of time for blame when your plane leaves after the regatta. We flew in I guess sixty people from Australia and others from around the world and set up a crisis control management center and a mission control. Then, in a very short period of time, we did a lot of stuff to that boat that improved it dramatically, redesigned it, and then raced it for the remainder of the trials."

Bertrand's team did not win. But they came closer than anyone else to beating the dominant New Zealand Challenge. In fact, they were the *only* team to take a race from the black boat. Ultimately *oneAustralia* had to settle for the runner-up position, a highly credible performance considering the disaster they had faced.

At Thomson Industries, John Thomson has spent a lot of time thinking about the parallels of flexibility in business and in sailing. And he has made a point of showing people in his business that there are lessons to be learned in sailing that they can take back to the workplace. "I love to show people what sailboat racing is all about and how you can apply it back to business—and even daily life. Sailing teaches you flexibility. In a sailboat race, if you're not flexible, you're not going to do well."

A big part of the game of sailing is playing the wind. On an upwind leg—that is a leg of the course where you must sail toward the oncoming wind—a sailboat must take an indirect route, zigzagging its way on a diagonal to the straight-line course. The reason for this is pure physics because, of course, no sailboat can sail directly toward the wind. The closest they can come is about forty degrees to the wind, using the sails and underwater foils to provide lifting power like an airplane wing. So, in a race, a tactician is faced with a choice: Do I go to the left side of the course first or to the right side? If the wind didn't shift, and was steady all over the racetrack, the answer would be easy—either way! But Mother Nature is the ultimate random number generator, and one thing a sailor learns very early is that the wind is hardly ever steady. So even small shifts in direction during the course of a race can provide the tactician an opportunity to cut the corner and sail a shorter distance!

The reason for this is geometry. If two boats sail off on opposite tacks for say ten minutes, and then the wind shifts a few degrees in a clockwise direction, the boat that went to the right side gets a big advantage. If there are no more shifts during that leg of the race, when the right-hand boat tacks over to converge with his enemy, he will be ahead—how much is a function of the separation of the boats and the magnitude of the wind shift, but it can be significant. A ten-degree clockwise shift will give that boat an immediate gain (on paper at least) of about 25 percent of the distance the boats are separated across the course. That's more of an advantage than any boat speed edge you could ever possess. It's like being on a boat twice the speed! Of course, like a gain in the stock market, you don't realize it until you "cash in," tack over, sail back across the course, and get between your competitor and the mark.

So a sailing tactician strives to gain any hint of which way the wind will shift. Weather forecasts can help, but often they are too much about the big picture. Tracking the movement of the wind on the water by watching the instruments and the heading of the boat can give one an idea of recent history, but most important is simply keeping an open eye ahead—watching other boats, flags on shore, the direction that the cows are facing in the field (really!)—anything to help see an upcoming wind shift!

At the Darden School, Drew Freides is learning all about the importance of flexibility in business. Says Freides, "One thing that they stress here in B-school is flexibility. We change business plans on the fly and—even in accounting—we are taught about flex-budgets, which are budgets that can be altered and manipulated in response to changing market conditions. In sailing I was always taught to be flexible. I always had a plan at the starting line, but very rarely did I actually fulfill that plan. That's because the playing field was constantly changing as wind gusts rolled across the course. I always had to keep an open mind to be flexible and change with the changing conditions. I think that has given me quite an advantage at school."

Before going back to school, Drew worked at Nelson/Marek Yacht Design in San Diego, one of the country's leading firms that design racing sailboats. Nelson/Marek has been involved in the "big leagues"—the America's Cup—since 1987. "It's important to keep your eyes wide open and your ear to the ground, and you have to consider the possible upsides and downsides of the different situations that develop. I look back at *Young America*'s 1995 America's Cup design team effort and that's really what drove our whole program. We began with an expected wind distribution—the conditions we expected to be racing in during the late winter and early spring in San Diego. Then we plugged those into the computer program that we used to develop our boat. Then we tried to estimate our competitors' boats and plug them into the program, too. We attempted to cover the whole range of scenarios, what we thought they'd do, how they would modify their boats, and so forth. Then the computer model would generate the predicted outcome of our boat versus theirs, in any given condition. It was impossible to have a boat that won in every race, because different boats excel in different conditions, but the goal of collecting all this data and then rigorously analyzing it was to optimize the odds of winning the majority of the races.

"In the business world, you can see how Barnes and Noble lost the race against Amazon.com because they were stuck in the old paradigm of a bricks-and-mortar bookstore. Instead of going in wholeheartedly, going after Amazon with everything they had, they used it as kind of a hedge, saying that on-line retail might be the way to go so let's get a stake in the ground and keep our stores in place. In this way, they've cannibalized sales out of their stores, yet they haven't really made a dent in Amazon at all. Amazon just seems to be crushing them."

Fortunately, many managers have seen the future of

business, and they are doing something about it. Rather than remaining stuck in the tired-out paradigms of the past, they are making fundamental changes to their businesses— changes that are setting the stage for phenomenal growth and success in the future. At Amway, Dick DeVos has led the charge to a new way of thinking.

DeVos explains, "What we're trying to create here is an atmosphere of nimbleness or an attitude that we're prepared to go where we need to go. Historically at this company, there's been a lot of inertia. While we've made minor adjustments in the course of things, it's been essentially the same basic business concept. Now, because of the introduction of technology and a real fundamental change in the competitive environment, we've had to look at our business in a new way and acknowledge that we're going to have to have a whole different attitude."

ConvergeNet's Dick Watts sees flexibility as a key element in a successful sailboat race, and in a successful business. According to Watts, "Sailing has so many variables in it. Every time you go out for a race it's a new beginning. You may have a great record and a boat that you believe is fast, but it really does start all over again with each race. You can never assume that what you did last time is going to work. And this energizes a 'start-from-a-fresh-clean-sheet' approach and encourages you to ensure that you're not doing anything by rote or routine or by force of habit. The concept of taking of a 'flyer' also comes from sailing and I think that can be an inspiration in business, too. If you are far behind, and it's the last race of the series, it may be time to throw the traditional rules of behavior out the window and do something that, under normal circumstances, may not have a very good chance of success. But since you have less to lose in that position, why not go for it and learn from it? It's a great way to keep everybody fresh and thinking about new ways of doing things.

"Take, for example, the way the Internet is changing the rules of the game and the valuations of some of these companies. People used to always think you have to have X amount of revenue and Y amount of profitability and other things fell into place from those basic drivers. But now we're finding that it's numbers of clicks and numbers of eyeballs and other parameters. Presumably what happened is that a few people took a flyer when that became their only option since they didn't have any revenue or profitability. And they started a whole new way of doing things."

View Change as an Opportunity

Is the glass half full, or half empty? A situation can be seen by some people optimistically—as an opportunity—while the exact same situation can be seen pessimistically—as a problem. Many employees see change as a problem, a threat to the status quo and to their well-being. Of course, for the many workers who joined the ranks of the down-sized, right-sized, and reengineered over the past decade, change literally *was* a threat to the status quo, and to their well-being.

While change in business does have its downside, the upside is vast. Every change opens up new products, new markets, new customers—and a raft of new businesses to address them. The opportunities that change creates for those who are willing to step up to them are indeed limitless. For long-established businesses, this creates great challenge, but also great potential.

Says DeVos, "Around here we really have to have a willingness to change, we've got to learn how to do 'new' better, how to do 'new' well. A lot of that is an attitude of getting rid of fear—fear of change—getting rid of resistance to change, and viewing change as an opportunity instead of a risk or a challenge.

"At the personal level, people need to understand that change poses opportunity for them in their day-to-day work and their jobs—it doesn't necessarily pose a risk to their security. Generally, the resistance tends to come from those who have either a greater financial or time investment or longevity at stake. The individuals in our organization who have been around for a longer time or have a particular position that suits them often view change as having more downside than upside.

"The challenge for us is to get the blood flowing among this more entrenched group—which is a very influential group in any organization—the leadership group. In our case, that's a small enough group that it's actually something we can impact. And that group in turn will set the atmosphere for the rest of the organization."

For many managers, developing a long-range business plan is a very painful and grueling process. It usually involves days, if not weeks, of time. Then it means committing to specific goals and milestones of performance for the future. Because of the very nature of the long-range planning process—and the aversion of many managers to go through it—the written plans that result tend to be static and unchanging. Consequentially, they become obsolete soon after they are drafted.

For Tom Whidden at North Marine Group, a business plan isn't something that should be filed away and forgotten. The best plans are those that are adjusted to reflect the changing environment, and that take advantage of the opportunities that change brings with it. Says Whidden, "The lesson I have learned is that you need to keep making decisions along the way. Writing a business plan for your business is like sailing a race—you amend it as you go along based on what you see is happening. If the boat you're racing against—in the present wind conditions—is going faster, you make a different decision than if you're going faster than he is. Same in business. If somebody's gaining on you or doing a little better job in one area, you change.

"We have a saying at North Sails, if it ain't broke, fix it anyway. Things are changing fast. We also say, control your own destiny or somebody else will. If you aren't trying to control as much of your destiny as you can, then you're continually being reactive rather than being proactive. It's exactly the same in a sailboat race and in business. If you're reacting to the other guy all the time, you're going to lose."

Why Do Companies Sponsor Sailboat Racing?

Hewlett-Packard (H-P) has been involved in the America's Cup as long as any company in the world. In the days before notebook computers were interfaced with sailing instruments on racing sailboats to manage, interpret, and record data, H-P's programmable calculators were part of every navigator's tool chest. In 1987, *Stars & Stripes* had an

H-P 71b programmable calculator interfaced with the sailing instruments and the telemetry system communicating with the support boats. By 1992, notebook computers were ubiquitous—used not only aboard Cup boats, but also grand-prix ocean racers. And today, computers are found throughout a Cup team, from the design group, to the sailors, to the office staff—literally everyone uses computers.

H-P has been a sponsor of America's Cup teams throughout this period, donating millions of dollars as well as hardware and resources to select teams. H-P's Vice President of Customer Efficacy, Alex Sozonoff, explains the three primary reasons why H-P is so committed to the America's Cup.

1. **Application of Technology.** "Just like our business customers, an America's Cup team operates in a very competitive and flexible environment—things happen all the time. And high technology is very important. I often compare Cup teams to Formula One auto racing teams in that regard. We have involved our supercomputers in the design process. We don't actually have one physical computer where the boats are being designed and built. It's all done by remote terminals. Of course, the more computing power the design team has, the more they can experiment with designs, running more iterations in their computer models in a fixed period of time. And there is also the application of information technology. It's a great showcase for our printers, our servers, and so forth. We can take a customer into *America One*'s (the team

H-P sponsored in the 2000 Cup campaign) office in San Francisco and show how a small company operates, because that's what a Cup team is. It's a small company in a very, very competitive environment."

2. **Client Entertainment.** "Sailing is one of the main interests of our target customers. The America's Cup is a great venue to take those customers—CEOs, CIOs, or even functional managers—the key people that make decisions that are critical for our business. And our salespeople tell us that no matter how inaccessible the client, once they have invited and entertained them at an America's Cup or a grand-prix race—spending some time relaxing together—suddenly there is a bond, and it's much easier to contact that particular customer afterward. And, of course, there is real value in bringing in our managers so they can have discussions with our key customers in a much more relaxed environment."

3. **Global Promotional Opportunities.** "Sailing in general, and the America's Cup in particular, is a global sport. This gives us some great leverage in terms of how we promote and advertise our involvement with the event. We developed a program which allows us to track business of the specific customers that we invited after the event. What I am looking for in the America's Cup is just a breakeven situation financially, because H-P will get all the other benefits that are harder to measure, such as impact on our reputation, image, and market share."

Chapter Seven

Rule Five —
Expect the Unexpected

In business, as in life, you can always expect the unexpected. Employees who quit and join your competition, customers that suddenly stop calling, computer networks that crash. If things always went the way you expected them to at work, they wouldn't call it "work."

The good news is that there are steps you can take to make your business life a lot more predict-able, and your unexpected surprises a lot fewer and farther in between. By taking the time up front to create goals and plans, and to be fully prepared for any possible outcome, it's guaranteed that your expectations will be met much more frequently than if you don't.

I spent nearly ten years racing on the professional match racing circuit. This series of events around the world experienced tremendous growth in the years immediately following our 1987 Cup victory in Australia. All the young aspiring skippers (myself included) saw the circuit as a way to establish a name in the sport. Since the America's Cup racing format is the same—match racing, with only two boats on the racetrack—a high ranking on the circuit increased your odds of being seen as a prospective Cup skipper.

The racing was intense—short thirty-minute sprints around a course in identical boats (usually thirty to forty feet in length with a five- to seven-person crew). The focus was on crushing the competition—beating them at the start and then staying ahead of them around the course. It didn't matter how much you won by as long as you won the race.

Since you rarely were more than a few boat lengths from the enemy, boat-for-boat tactics were of paramount importance. Like a game of chess, for every move there was a countermove, but you had to keep in mind your position relative to the next turning mark and the phasing of the wind, too. As the circuit evolved, the tactics became much more complex as we sailors learned how better to use the rules (and often the bow of our boats) as a weapon.

My tactician, Moose McClintock, and I developed a system for dealing with the myriad of moves our competitor might make out on the racecourse. As you would expect, on shore we analyzed races and discussed possible tactics for hours. During a race, we kept up a regular dialogue about the possible moves and countermoves that could occur. That way, we were more prepared to make a quick reaction to any change of course by our competitor. Nevertheless, sometimes the action was so fast and furious that we simply had to rely on our instincts—there was no time for discussion. And it was not uncommon to come home with a big hole in your boat. Racing in Perth's beautiful Swan River, we even made it onto the NBC "Today" show for one dramatic high-speed crash with Australia's Peter Gilmour. But whenever possible we made ourselves more ready with conversations like this:

> "Okay, right now if he jibes we want to let him go, and get our wind behind him before jibing. But in a couple of minutes, we'll be nearly at layline and then we want to lead him in, or at least go simultaneous."
>
> "But do you think the wind is strong enough to keep an overlap all the way in if he rolls us?"
>
> "No, not yet, let's keep fighting for the inside—that's our goal."

Having these conversations really helped reduce the pressure on me, the helmsman, because I felt more ready and had the benefit of input from Moose—something I would not have time to get after our competitor did jibe. In short, we were more prepared, no matter how unexpected our competitor's tactics.

Have a Game Plan

It has been shown time and time again that people with plans—regardless of how simple or elaborate they might be—have a higher probability of achieving their goals than do people who do not have plans. This fact was proven in a landmark study of Yale University graduates. In 1953, researchers polled the graduating class of Yale University and found that only 3 percent of the graduates made a regular practice of setting goals and putting them into writing. When the researchers returned in 1973 to see how the Yale class of '53 had fared, the 3 percent of graduates who had set goals and put them into writing had amassed a fortune more than all the other 97 percent of their classmates combined. While not every goal that we set will have such a dramatic impact on our lives, the power of setting goals is undeniable.

America's Cup winner Bill Koch considers plans, goals, and objectives to be the foundation of any successful endeavor—whether it's in sailing or in business. Koch applied this framework to his Cup-winning 1992 *America³* campaign. "To begin, we set some very clear objectives. For example, we said our purpose out here is to win. Next, we did a complete analysis of what it had taken during the Cup's one-hundred-and-forty-one-year history to win and came to some really nonobvious conclusions. We learned that a slow boat has never won—only a fast boat wins. Secondly, the team that wins is the one that makes the least mistakes, not the one that is the most brilliant.

"So we said, 'Okay, what we're going to do is we're going to have two criteria by which we judge everything. Criteria number one is does it make the boat faster, and criteria number two is does it make the crew better? And if it doesn't meet those two criteria—no matter how good the idea is—we're not going to do it.' During an America's Cup competition, you get a lot of miscellaneous stuff thrown at you. Go to this party, make this speech, and so forth, but we continuously judged every possible activity by those two criteria. If it didn't make the boat faster or it didn't make the crew better, then it was out. We tried to have everybody in the organization think that way so they'd allocate their time and energy and efforts on either of those two things.

"In big business, people often allocate their time and energy to things that may be the prerogatives of their specific little group, and not the organization as a whole. Or if the goals of the organization are too complicated and not simple enough so everybody can understand them and embrace them, then each little group in the organization develops its own goals for its own benefit. A big difference between the America's Cup and business is that you can define your goal extremely simply—it's to win the Cup. In business, it's much harder, and it's much more of an intellectual challenge.

"The other thing about the America's Cup is you have only a limited time period to do it all in, whereas in business you can stretch things out longer and longer and longer. Nevertheless, the discipline should still apply. You should be able to set very clear goals and, in addition, you should be able to set very strict time requirements or milestones for yourself. If you don't, things will tend to drift aimlessly, or drift according to the wishes of the senior management or the ruling elite."

Norwood Davis, chairman of the board and CEO of Trigon Healthcare, Inc., agrees that it's critically important for organizations to have plans and strategies—not only to help the organization and its employees attain their goals but also to ensure that all employees are working *with* one another rather than *against* one another. Says Davis, "A critical part of any strategy—particularly for the *execution* of any strategy—is to have a clear and easily understood goal which is very obvious. I refer to this as the end game. It's important to make sure that everybody understands the end game and is focused on achieving it. Three or four years ago we were in the process of converting this company from a mutual insurance company to a stock company with a public offering. We were one of the first in the industry to do this, so there was not a lot of precedent for it—not a whole lot of history we could draw on.

"There were a number of very complicated, confusing factors: regulatory issues, legal considerations, Wall Street issues, as well as public hearings, delays, and more. I'm convinced that, without the constant focus on the end game—namely, getting the public offering done and providing us access to capital—we just wouldn't have gotten it done. The same thing applies in racing a sailboat as well: What's the end game? If you have a boat you've got to beat, what are you doing relative to that boat? What's your plan to win or to achieve your end game—not what's happening right around you at that particular point in time."

Of course, Mr. America's Cup, Dennis Conner, *always*

has a plan. In fact if there's one thing you can be sure of, he always has *lots* of plans. As we write this book, he is putting the finishing touches on plans for his eighth America's Cup campaign. At the same time, Dennis is beginning plans for his next challenge in the Volvo Ocean Race, which will follow the Cup a year later. On top of that, he continues to campaign his Etchells (a thirty-foot one-design sloop that attracts some of the best sailors in the world) on the international circuit.

But just because Dennis Conner has a plan, it doesn't mean that he's going to publicize it to the whole world. Says Conner of his effort for America's Cup 2000, "Even back in 1995, right after the Kiwis won, I had a plan. But I knew the event was five years away, that it was crazy to start beating on my chest and saying how I was going to win the America's Cup and hire marketing people, and PR people, and office staff—like many of my competitors have—and waste millions of dollars when there was really nothing they could do. There's no way you were going to sell anything that far out from the Cup, corporate America doesn't work that way. So I saw my competitors go through millions and millions and millions of dollars and they had nothing to show from it. I kept my mouth shut until it was time to start going to work, and I saved all that money."

Tom Whidden, president of North Marine Group, is another big fan of plans. According to Tom, "Plans help you allocate the two most important commodities of all in any organization—time and money. Most people would probably say money first, but your most precious commodity in an America's Cup campaign is really time. Money comes after, because you could have all the money in the world and only have two months to go. Kind of like having a bad sickness and winning the lottery two months before you're going to die.

"We're going through a little strategic planning session right now in our business and one of the things we're realizing is that it isn't just profit and loss. It's return on equity, it's how you utilize your resources, it's the amount of people you've got to do a given job. They're all important to the ultimate success of a business. You have to set goals for yourself along the way to measure how you're doing."

Consultant Doug Stewart makes a living showing people the benefits of planning ahead. He says, "At our Caribbean Challenge, we did a lot of strategic planning. We noticed, for example, that if we sailed a forty-four-footer like a dinghy, we had an edge on our competition because we would take immediate advantage of a mistake. And we looked ahead. 'If they do this, this is what we're going to do. And if they do this, this is what we're going to do.' That way we didn't have to have a team meeting every time our competitor tacked to decide how to respond. We also decided in advance who was going to make the decisions. We had one fellow, Neil, who was quite good on strategies, so if we had any debate on strategy, he had the final word. It made things move a lot quicker."

And while the competition was off enjoying their time in an exotic locale, Doug's team was already making plans for the next day's racing. "We would sit together in the evening while the other people were partying and have our strategic planning meetings for the next day's racing. Here's what the course looks like, here's the kind of race it is, what do we need to think about?"

Kurt Antonius

Senior Manager, Public Relations

AMERICAN HONDA MOTOR COMPANY, INC.

There are many, many variables we can control while sailing—choice of sail and trim, boat heading, balance, equipment, choice of crew, etc. There are even more variables we *cannot* control—wind direction and velocity, wave height and direction, current, reefs, landmass, and so on. Constantly changing conditions, equipment breakdowns, rapid changes in weather, and other unpredicted changes require us to adapt quickly and have a solid backup plan. It is the same in the marketplace. We can control many elements of our business strategy, but there are an infinite number of conditions we cannot change—economic conditions, currency fluctuations, competitor actions, consumer trends, government regulations, etc. To succeed, one must have a solid strategy, adapt quickly, and always have a backup plan—more than likely, you will need it.

Be Prepared

While sailing in the Olympic Pre-Trials aboard my three-person Soling class sloop, I had an experience that hammers home the concept of preparation. It was the final race of the series and we were leading the regatta. One more good race and we would have achieved the biggest win of our

Olympic Campaign. About five minutes after the start, we were sailing along in good breeze and in a good position when all of a sudden there was a loud "bang" and the mainsail started flapping. It took a moment to see that a fitting that held the sail's control rope (the mainsheet) had come apart. The problem was a tiny, little ten-cent metal pin that had fallen out.

Fortunately, I had learned a great jury-rigging trick while sailing ocean racers the previous year. I asked my middle-man, Dave Perry, to grab the Vice-Grip pliers out of the tool bag. We then trimmed the mainsheet in back so the sail was set properly and I clamped the Vice-Grips on the rope just where it came from the boom. That took the load off the broken fitting and gave Dave time to find the tiny pin in the bilge of our boat and put everything back together while I drove. We ended up third place in that race—good enough to win the U.S. Olympic Pre-Trials.

Preparation is a key element of success for almost any business venture. Without a doubt, there is a direct and measurable relationship between the amount of preparation that you do, and your ultimate success. Not only will you have all the facts that you need at your disposal but you will have run through a variety of possible scenarios—and ways to counter problems that might come up along the way. And, perhaps most important, the more prepared you are, the more confident you'll be, and this confidence will make you more effective in your abilities and in your job.

John Burnham & Company's Malin Burnham puts preparation near the top of his list of most important sailboat racing—and business—rules. He truly believes that, if you prepare hard enough, and well enough, no one will be able to keep you from achieving your goals—whether it's winning the America's Cup, or landing a new insurance client. Says Burnham, "When we go out to make a presentation for an investment sale, it takes a lot of preparation. And you know, I can relate that to every sailing campaign I've ever been involved in. You just don't go out to the starting line and dust off your boat and go sailing—not if you want to win. And you can't do that either when you're making presentations. The buildup to a race is the same thing as getting a presentation together, or brokering a sale for a tenant to take a long-term lease on a lot of space. You have to be prepared."

Gary Jobson on Leading a Crew (and a Business)

Gary Jobson is regarded as one of the most vocal promoters of the sport of sailing. He is also a world-class sailor who has won many championships in One Design classes; the America's Cup with Ted Turner in 1977, the infamous; he's also won the Fastnet Race, and many of the world's ocean races. He is well known as ESPN's resident sailing expert and has covered every America's Cup since 1983 for the network.

Here is his list of the ways that you can lead a group of sailors—and businesspeople—to success:

* Develop and articulate your strategy. Execute it with precision. Share it with everyone. Get everyone

on the same page. Prompt attendance at meetings is mandatory. Try to forecast tricky situations to prepare the crew.

✳ Remain calm when the going gets tough.

✳ Spell everything out. Have clear goals, communications, and assignments.

✳ Keep everyone fresh. Burnout produces mistakes.

✳ Follow your gut when making decisions. Second guessing breaks down the command structure.

✳ Consult others only to a point. Ask for strategy input before the event, not in the heat of competition. Be a leader, not a consensus builder. Sell ideas, don't dictate.

✳ Compliment. Everyone responds to proper acknowledgment of accomplishments.

✳ Understand what makes your systems work, including the abilities of your team.

Keep Your Head Out of the Boat

Have you ever been so caught up in some small issue that you neglected to see the big picture? In business, it happens all the time. Maybe you were so focused on improving your revenues that you failed to notice that profitability had dropped into the tank. Or perhaps you were so busy catching up on performance appraisals that you forgot to thank a team of employees for the many weeks of late nights they put in on a new business proposal. Or you might have thought your customers were more interested in saving a few pennies, when what they really were concerned about was the declining quality of your products.

Norwood Davis, chairman & CEO of Trigon Healthcare, has witnessed at close hand the danger of having too narrow a perspective—both in his business, and on the water. Davis says, "You've got to keep your head out of the boat, whether you're skippering a boat, running a business, or running a division. It seems so obvious, but too often we get so focused on a critical issue or the specifics of the job, we don't see what's happening—whether it's changes in the marketplace, what customers want, what the competition's doing, any number of other things. When you're racing, some people on the boat have jobs that are focused inward, like the trimmers who make sure the sails are set right or the bow person who sees that the boat is prepared for the next turning mark, but there are some key people aboard who have got to keep their heads out of the boat. When you're steering the boat, it's awfully easy to just constantly look at what's going on onboard—things like boat speed and the preparedness of your crew can take up all your focus. But you've also got to keep your eye on the other boats. You've got to make sure that you're sailing as fast as they are, and that they're not on a better course than you are."

Not letting distractions prevent you from seeing the big picture is what this point is really all about. It's easy to get so distracted with every little thing going on aboard your boat that you don't look around the racetrack as much as you should. But on the flip side, for the helmsman and other members of a big-boat crew, getting your head out of the boat and looking around can also be distracting—but somebody has to do it! On some boats, the teams divide up the responsibilities so that the helmsman's primary goal is steering the boat and maximizing boat speed in concert with the sail trimmers who share that duty. Then someone sitting out on the rail will be assigned the job of watching the boat's performance relative to the nearby competition and feed that information to the driver. Another person may be watching the water close ahead to warn the driver of waves and upcoming gusts of wind. The tactician will be responsible for looking farther afield—at the fleet and the wind up the course—to try and pick the best course for the boat. But in tight situations, such as mark roundings, the helmsman has to be able to shift gears and weave the boat through the mayhem. At that point, there is no right way to divide up responsibilities—just make sure someone on your crew has his or her head out of the boat!

Former Delaware governor Pete du Pont tells a sailboat racing story about the danger of just focusing close aboard. Du Pont says, "It is really important to get your head out of the boat and to look at the big picture. You've got to look at the jib and you've got to look at the waves when you're going to windward, you've got to feel the heel, but you've also got to look at the big world. I've got a picture of my J44 *Glory* sailing along in a sea in which there's not a whitecap—it's not even close to being whitecaps—and the boat has the heavy number-one headsail set. You look at that picture and you wonder, 'Why is that—shouldn't they have a lighter weight sail up in those moderate conditions?' And I remember—this was in a Chicago to Mackinac Race on Lake Michigan and we were sailing along to windward. The wind speed on our instruments was reading around eight to ten knots, and then it began to climb. Pretty soon it was ten and a half, eleven, twelve, and finally it got up over twelve and we said, without ever looking at the sea, 'Man, we better change down to that heavy one.' We relied on the instruments and found out later on that an electrical discharge had fried the wind sensor at the top of the mast so we were getting bad data. We had changed our sail because we looked only at the instruments and not at the real world. We sailed for an hour with the wrong jib before somebody finally said, 'Hey, where are the whitecaps? It can't be blowing fourteen out here.' You've got to get your head out of the boat!"

United Technologies' Chairman and CEO George Davis is direct about what he thinks about competition. He likes it. "It's, after all, the incentive for each of us to get better. It's what lifts the human condition, and as long as it's healthy and constructive and played by the rules, it works and works well. I've always liked the phrase 'bloodless warfare.' It's an apt description of business and it's an apt description of the racecourse. But, it's also true that we have competitors we like to race against and those we don't. The discriminator is good clean competition played by the rules. There are people on the racecourse I would just as soon stay away from, and others I don't mind getting right up next to. The same is true in business, good clean competition makes everybody better. You like to respect your competitor in both domains. If he wins, it's because he's better, and you just take that lesson and go back and work harder and do better yourself the next time.

"Benchmarking has been a really important practice in business over the last fifteen years. We also have great security analysts in our country, and the combination of these two has been a great force for improvement for most companies. We're no exception at UTC, and I can't emphasize enough the influence of both on us. We do have a defined set of about a dozen peer companies, people like us, Allied-Signal, General Electric, Emerson, Textron, Boeing. The security analysts measure us, and we measure ourselves. It's just like the race course, you get a scorecard every time, and it's the basis for targeting improvements, for running the enterprise. [Author's note: David didn't say it, but UTC is number one among its dozen peers in total shareholder return over the last five years.] Competition does this, competition is key, competition makes us all better, and that's a useful goal."

Amway's Dick DeVos knows that if you get too comfortable in your current markets and with your current customers, you can miss out on tremendous opportunities—opportunities that are simply waiting to be recognized and acted on. "My biggest contribution to the Amway business has been the movement to global enterprise. That took us from very much a U.S.-based company to one where seventy percent of our sales are now outside the United States. For many, all they saw was risk. In their minds, the United States was a big enough market, and why would we want to go to all these other places? And all I saw were opportunities. I said, 'My goodness, just look at the population numbers, just look at the economics. The United States has the largest single economy, but if you add up everybody else all together, they dwarf us.' In my view, the U.S. side of our business should be twenty percent of the total, and the international ought to be eighty percent of the total. We're close now—we're thirty–seventy."

Mark Landwer

Vice President of National Accounts, Hartford Computer Group, Inc., Inverness, Illinois

Business

Over the last two years, the computer "reseller" industry has gone through tremendous change. Many companies, including the Hartford Computer Group, Inc. (HCG), have been compelled to develop new core businesses in response to these market forces. Changing direction, however, in a $500 million company cannot be done overnight. As a matter of fact, it has taken HCG eighteen months to develop a solid game plan and come up with our new core business offering. During this time, our company struggled because of the change in the industry. Our management team knew we had to change direction—from a hardware company to a service company—but they didn't know how. We lost focus and, even though we tried just about everything we could think of to spur sales, our numbers kept sliding downward. Our divisions were going different directions and everyone was trying to do one another's job. We did not convey that we were in control or had a game plan that we believed in. Within the last sixty days, our management staff developed a three-step plan that will be our future. The plan was conveyed downward through the corporate ladder and everyone understood and believed in it. Never before has our company had the direction and focus it has now. Our sales are up, and our organization is stronger than ever!

SAILING

Our tactician, Ron Brinckerhoff, is relatively new in his position—he has been sailing his entire life, but has been calling tactics for only the past two years. Last weekend, I noticed something very important. Our boat is always very fast, and we work well as a team during the first leg of any given race. Ron always has a game plan before the start and he is very confident in his approach. He communicates the plan effectively to the crew, he is confident, and relatively calm. As the race progresses, however, you cannot always stick to your beginning game plan—the variables change too much. When this happens, Ron starts to second guess himself. He complains, and starts asking the crew basic questions about what he should do. Once this happens, the crew lose confidence in him, and they lose concentration on their jobs as everyone pipes in to make suggestions. Sure enough, as soon as this happens, we start dropping back in the fleet. This shows just how important a game plan is. If you have a plan, you have to get people to believe in it. When you accomplish that, both the employees in an organization, and the crew on a sailboat, will have faith in you and focus on their jobs.

*"A ship in harbor is safe,
but that's not what
ships are built for."*

—John A. Shedd

Chapter Eight

Rule Six —
Push the Limits

From September 1997 until May 1998, nine boats took part in an epic adventure—a race around the world. It was the seventh Whitbread Around the World Race (the 2001–2 race will be run again under a new name—the Volvo Ocean Race). Run every four years, the race has become increasingly more serious and more professional. In the first few Whitbreads, crews raced on boats that you would be happy living on with your family. They were big, comfortable, solid craft with all the comforts of home. Some of the teams even had a cook on board! Today's Whitbread has a very different look.

The ten- to twelve-person crews race sixty-five-foot stripped-out racing machines optimized for fast ocean sailing. The amenities (and the cooks!) have all but disappeared in the quest for speed. For example, to save weight, the crews eat freeze-dried camping food—for weeks on end. The only qualification for a cook on one of these boats is being able to boil water. Speaking of which, water is made daily by a generator-powered water maker. If that piece of equipment breaks—as it did for the American crew on *Chessie* several days from the tip of Cape Horn—all of a sudden, your food supply is virtually inedible. Luckily some of the crew aboard had squirreled away some chocolate bars for snacks. Can you imagine subsisting on rations of chocolate bars and rainwater for nearly a week—while performing an athletic endeavor around the clock in near freezing temperatures?

The racecourse has nine legs, with short breaks on shore for teams to recuperate before moving on. Starting in England, the course takes the fleet south—to South Africa—and then around the globe to the east. Much of the sailing takes place in the famed Southern Ocean (the general term for that band of water that girdles the globe just north of Antarctica and South of all other continents), where the westerly winds blow at gale-force intensity and the waves build up to astronomical size as there is no land mass in these latitudes to hold them back. I have sailed in the Southern Ocean once—for all of about one hour—when we made a "gentleman's" rounding of Cape Horn on Skip Novak's sloop *Pelagic* while filming a special for ESPN. We peeked out around the corner from the protection of a group of islands we had been cruising through in our exploration of Tierra del Fuego's vast network of protected waterways, and it looked cold and gray. And we were there on a good day—the wind was "only" blowing thirty-five knots and the waves were "only" ten feet high. Of course it was unseasonably "warm," too—maybe forty-five degrees!

During the last Whitbread, I became hooked on the daily reports E-mailed in real time off the race boats via satellite communication. John Bertrand's Quokka Sports created an amazing Web site where you could follow the race closely from the comfort of your own home. Some of my favorite reports were written by one of the youngest members of the crew of *Toshiba*, Kelvin Harrap. Here is one of my favorites—it gives you an idea of life on board a sixty-five-foot race boat, surfing down big gray waves in the Southern Ocean.

Toshiba *Daily Report 12/2/98*

LIFE IN THE SOUTHERN OCEAN

I am shaken awake at midnight—time to go on deck. A quick look in the navigation room shows the wind has been gusting to 38 knots, steady at 30 knots and we have our spinnaker up. The first thing I think about is how I have to drive in twenty minutes and I do not enjoy this stuff. A quick cup of coffee and put some wet wet-weather gear on. Safety harnesses are a must in these conditions as there are two tons of water rushing over the deck at 25 knots, you get washed off your feet all the time.

Jeff Scott, the hit man, is at the helm as usual asking for more sail area. "He's really gone mad" I think to myself and try not to show how nervous I am, but really I am shit scared. I take the helm from Scotty and after a few minutes start to settle in and even enjoy it a little more. Driving in these conditions requires total concentration as being caught even 1 or 2 degrees off course or hit by a bad wave would be costly not only to the boat and sails but to people as well. But the picture has changed now from a pleasant 25 to 30 to a scary 30 to 38 knots. I am thinking how I would love to get this chute off but also know the other guys (on the other boats) are pushing hard too. We are reaching speeds of 27 knots screaming down the huge waves. You can not see the instruments and there are people scrambling to stay on their feet.

Then suddenly a massive wave comes over the deck throwing Alan and Steve into the steering wheel—I was washed to the end of my safety line and off the wheel. I scramble back to the wheel to try to keep the boat from broaching only to find Alan's head through the wheel. I had to kick him out of the way just to save the wipe out.

Back on the helm, the wind is a little lighter but we have a new problem, a tangle of rope on the winch. The boys can not free it. I am trying to stay calm, but the wind is back up to 37 knots. They are trying to lead a new sheet and do that. But next, the cover of the new spinnaker sheet breaks so we can not ease the sheet out and this time I lose control a little on a bad wave—so the spinnaker flogs, but we get back on course only to find there are now no ropes at all on the spinnaker and it is all hands on deck to get it down. Of course it comes down in shreds so Nick and Daniel spend the next three days repairing the spinnaker.

Down below, the heater has now broken and Capey (the navigator) reckons he has an iceberg on the bow which he has spotted on the radar. Thankfully it's just *Merit Cup* (another competitor). With Ross at the helm the next day we sail past. It was a spectacular sight—two Whitbread 60s screaming along at 25 knots only 4 boat lengths apart!

Well everyone is very tired and cold but know we have only a few more days in this hell hole until we round Cape Horn. Someone please get a gun and threaten me with death if you hear me talking about doing this race again.

Kelvin

As the Whitbread Around the World Race (now named the Volvo Ocean Race) has garnered more attention within the sailboat racing community—and with sponsors who are lining up to pump more and more money into the teams that brave this exciting, but treacherous, journey—it has increasingly become a proving ground for the most advanced sailing technology available today. Not only are these sailors pushing the limits of human performance, each and every day of the race, but their equipment is pushing the limits of current sailing technology so the pressure is on to make every winch, every mast, every hull—and every part in between—lighter, stronger, and more streamlined. This requires incredible creativity, an ability to seamlessly integrate the latest technological advances into the boat, and lots of money. To do anything less is to concede the race before it even begins.

To win the race, businesses have to push the limits—they have to become lighter, stronger, and more streamlined. Creativity and innovation have to be encouraged, nurtured, and then put into practice. Organizations—and the men and women within them—have to be willing to take risks, and their managers have to learn to reward risk-taking behavior rather than punishing it. Persistence pays—both on the water and off—and those companies that stay in the race and continue to push the limits until they cross the finish line are the ones who will reap the sweet rewards of success.

In this chapter, we'll explore just what it means to push the limits, and how some of the nation's top businesspeople do just that.

Innovate—Be Creative

Innovation and creativity are the wellspring of progress in organizations. Every product can be improved; every service can be provided to customers and clients better, more efficiently, and more effectively; every customer can experience an even better relationship with your firm and its employees. Innovation and creativity allow you and your employees to constantly push the limits of the status quo, and find ever-better ways to serve your customers and your shareholders.

But as much as we all know the critical need for creativity in the workplace, it seems that many organizations have yet to get with the program. Where companies in Japan expect (and get) their employees to make *hundreds* of suggestions to improve work processes each and every year, in the United States, companies receive an average of one suggestion per *seven* employees per year! Is it because employees are any less creative in the United States? Of course not. We believe the reason is because not enough managers sincerely value employee innovation and creativity, preferring instead employees who do what they are told and rock the boat as little as possible.

DynaYacht's Chuck Robinson believes that his ability to be creative is the one overriding reason for his tremendous business success. Says Robinson, "Being creative is important—there's no reason to exist if you're not creating. For me, technological innovations that have commercial potential are my form of creativity. I always ask this question: 'If you're not bound by tradition, and you step back, is there a better way of doing it?'

"Nike has been creative from the very beginning, too. At the time, Adidas and Puma controlled the running shoe market. Then Nike came in from left field and completely changed the concept of how you produce running shoes, and how you market them—tying in with professional athletes. I've been involved with Nike since 1971, and I've learned a *lot* about innovation from them. I'm now chairman of the finance committee, and in every board meeting we talk about innovative, creative things that we want to do.

"For instance, I've been pushing a new concept of having untended booths in malls where you can go in and you push buttons and on the video monitor you'll see various tennis shoes. When you decide what shoe you want to buy, then you stand on a lighted plate and it automatically records your foot size—actually, both feet, because they're very often quite different. You punch in the style and color of the shoe you want, you put in your credit card, and it electronically transmits the order to our Memphis, Tennessee, headquarters. They box the order, charge it to your credit card, and drop it off at Federal Express, which is just a few blocks away. It's delivered to your house the next day and you never have to set foot in a store."

Ross Ritto has been involved in the music and entertainment business for decades. His company, Southern California Sound Image, Inc., has done the audio production for Jimmy Buffett's tours since the early seventies and has grown to be one of the largest audio production companies in the country, producing tours for, among others, Crosby, Stills, and Nash, Melissa Etheridge, Dan Fogelberg, Bonnie Raitt, and Brian Wilson, to name a few. Ross is also into racing sailboats—he currently owns the forty-foot sloop *High Five*, which consistently finishes in the money in regattas throughout Southern California.

His interest in sailing and the construction of boats led him into innovating and developing a technology that is revolutionizing his industry—composites. Says Ross, "One of the big things with the industry that I'm in is speaker enclosures. We go into an arena and hang them above the stage. So for years and years, I've been working at these concerts looking up at three or four tons' worth of speaker enclosures just dangling there thinking, 'Man, I hope nothing happens to that tonight.'

"At the same time I was noticing the way a modern racing boat is built. Now a sailboat hull really needs to be both stiff and lightweight. And among other things, a speaker enclosure really needs to be stiff. So I decided to experiment with building speaker enclosures using the same materials they build a sailboat out of. And for the first couple of years it was a pretty miserable attempt because I was learning it all myself since I couldn't afford to hire a composites expert. But I just kept playing around with the idea. After we built them, we'd bring these various experimental speaker enclosures—that by now were becoming very lightweight—to a friend of mine who is an acoustics expert and he'd keep saying, 'No, that's no good.'

"Up until then I had always used foam core. But the foam was just transferring all the vibrations through the box and making it acoustically worse than a piece of wood. That's when we tried using Nomex core [the same honeycomb core used in the construction of America's Cup boats]. The Nomex core acted like an airspace between these two skins and something pretty phenomenal happened to the box. While the interior vibrated, the outside was just as stiff as anything. You could put your hand on it when there was just tons of volume going through it, and it wouldn't vibrate. So now we actually have been awarded an application and a methods patent for building speaker enclosures out of the same kind of materials they use in racing sailboats. We employ carbon and fiberglass skins with a Nomex core.

"When I first started experimenting with it, all my employees thought I was nuts because I'd be back there in the shop with a paint brush painting fiberglass and stuff. But after we actually proved this, we brought one of our boxes to JBL—the largest manufacturer of speaker enclosures in the world—and they did all these laser tests on it and immediately came back to us and said 'You guys have got a really good idea here.' And today, we have a licensing agreement with them to provide speaker enclosures."

That good idea and the persistence that Ross had to experiment and innovate have resulted in the creation of a second company—Audio Composite Engineering, Inc., which is producing high-tech speaker boxes for commercial and consumer applications. And today, when Sound Image hangs speakers before a Jimmy Buffett concert, they weigh less than half of what they weighed before!

Manage Risk

Risk is a two-edged sword. Not enough risk, and your organization isn't growing, it isn't moving—and it will soon find itself in the doldrums, overtaken by faster-moving competitors. Too much risk, and your company can be torn to shreds. The ideal situation is to find a balance between too much and too little risk, a balance where you're pushing the limits—and maybe even enduring a failure or two—but where you're not betting the entire financial well-being of your organization and its employees and shareholders on a particularly risky strategy. The place where this balance exists is different for every organization—it's up to you to get a feel for where it's at, and then to orient your people around it.

As chairman and CEO of Trigon Healthcare, a major part of Norwood Davis's job is the management of risk. According to Davis, "Managing risk is a core skill, a core capability for our business, but it applies in any business and so it does with racing. There's no question in our business: Those who manage risk the best over a period of time win. But there's a huge difference between managing risk and avoiding risk. Managing risk means that you have a lot of information, a lot of data, a lot of knowledge, a lot of experience, and a lot of talent. You know you have these skills, you know what you know, and know what you don't know. You know where the risks are and you know what the opportunities and the rewards are for that—you know there's a downside and you try and understand what that downside is.

"In our business over the last five or ten years, there has been a lot of new competition in this business from HMOs, hospitals founding their own health plans, and a number of other arrangements. Some of these entities grew very rapidly and very successfully, and Wall Street would tell us, 'Geez, why don't you be like those guys?' But you know what? Virtually every one of those newcomers has blown up. I'm convinced that a big reason for that is they didn't realize—or perhaps didn't want to acknowledge—that this is a risk business and they just didn't have the core skills or talent to manage the risk.

"And, again, that applies to sailboat racing. I am convinced that, over a long period of time, those skippers who are good at risk management will separate from the rest of the pack. And those risks can be anything from which side of the course to be on, to the approach of the mark, to crossing the starting line, to which sails to use.

"Last July, we were about to report that for six straight quarters—our first six quarters as a public company—we had exceeded Wall Street's estimates in earnings, which was huge for us. We were performing at a high level, and I concluded that the balance of '99 looked really good. At that point it would have been very easy to feel good about where we were but, frankly, this industry is in a bit of turmoil and changing very rapidly. I didn't think anybody could evaluate what would be happening in the year 2000 and beyond.

"So I analogized our situation to my staff this way. I said, 'It's like you're racing a sailboat and everything is going great. You're in the lead, the boat's trimmed up—everything's in the zone. You're on the right side of the course, but a mile or two up the course there's this fog bank rolling in and now's the time to get it together—now's the time to do what you've got to do to outperform everyone else in this fog bank. So you immediately plot your position and figure out exactly where the finish line is and where your competition is, all the things that are a hell of a lot easier to do in bright sunshine and visibility. By making that extra effort, you eliminate as much risk as you can when you've got it all together rather than waiting to see if that fog bank is going to lift before it hits you. It's all about trying to eliminate as much risk as you can when you're in conditions that are most favorable.' "

One of the things that you must learn to be a successful tactician on the race course—and this applies just the same on a single-handed dinghy as it does on a seventy-foot maxi-boat—is the concept of managing risk. To do so one must fully understand the "game theory" of the sport. This involves gaining an appreciation for the potential gains and losses that can accrue when you sail on the opposite tack— away from your competitors—as you zig-zag your way against the wind to a mark. Some of those gains and losses can be attributed to differences in wind velocity (usually, more is better) or differences in the flow of currents. By learning a bit about local-scale meteorology, you can increase your ability to predict those wind changes. For example, wind blowing parallel to the shore will increase at a point or headland. And some of these gusts and lulls can actually be seen when you train your eyes to look for color variations on the surface of the water caused by ripples.

One of the most easily understood principles in the game of sailing strategy is the effect of wind shifts on two boats that are separated (more leverage) across the racecourse. In fact, it can all be reduced to a mathematical problem, using geometry to predict how a change in wind will affect the relative position of two boats. In ocean racing, teams will use a computer running a program called a route optimizer to calculate the best course to take based upon an assumed set of conditions—a weather and current-flow forecast. Of course, just as is the case with any other computer program, it's only as accurate as the data it is crunching. As any sailor knows, however, it is impossible to get a hundred percent accurate forecast of the wind. And on a small, twenty-minute leg in a buoy race, no weather forecast is going to be able to help you. Therefore, you try to see trends based upon the conditions you are experiencing right now on the racecourse, and you keep in mind the geometric principles of leverage. That way, when you make an educated guess about which way to go, it is tempered with the understanding of how much risk you are assuming.

Mike Spence, former dean of Stanford University's Graduate School of Business, can see the parallels between risk-taking behavior in sailboat racing and in business. According to Spence, "In sailboat racing, there's a lot of maneuvering where one boat is trying to stay in front of the other guy. But there are times when it pays to leave the competition and take chances. A lot of those sorts of tactical and strategic calculations are in some very general sense similar to the kinds of things that business people do. Sometimes you have to take a chance because it's the only way to get past somebody. And sometimes you have to avoid taking chances because you're already in the driver's seat."

One of the things every sailor must learn is the principle of conservative sailing. There is a time and a place for bucking the odds and sailing to a completely different side of the course than the rest of your competition, but it is *not* at the beginning of a regatta when the scoreboard is blank. The game of sailing rewards the sailor who stays with the fleet, who waits for them to make the mistake rather than constantly going for the gold and risking falling hopelessly out of touch with the competition.

Human nature, it seems, doesn't work that way. Something in the human brain wants the big glory—to win the race by miles. We all want to make a clearly remarkable decision that will have a profound and obvious impact on the outcome of the race. But there's no such thing as a free lunch—in sailing or in life. If you go for the gold all the time, and roll the dice in every race, the odds against you are long. In sailing, we call that risky strategy "banging the corner." It may feel good to be headed out there all alone—especially if you are already a little bit behind the leaders—but twenty minutes later it can feel pretty lonely sailing back in toward the mark, watching the entire fleet cross your bow.

MBA student Drew Freides has also found his way to Wall Street, and he has learned that his prospective employers are *very* interested in his risk management experience—most of which he learned from racing sailboats. "Interestingly, sailing came up during interviews for my summer job on Wall Street. Once they learned I was a sailor, people started asking me questions about risk management and how important it is in racing. There's no question that sailing has really taught me how to optimize odds—to know when I've got an upside and to consolidate, or when I've got a downside, to limit my losses and try to dig my way back slowly.

"When you're racing against a fleet of boats, you spend your entire time assessing the playing field because currents, wind direction, and velocity are constantly changing. If you are ahead of somebody or in a favorable position in the fleet you learn to consolidate—you tack and cross an entire fleet and become a little conservative once you have that favorable position. You make sure you maintain that position, instead of extending and really going for the big win. Why? Because it really doesn't matter if you win by a second or you win by a minute as long as you win. On Wall Street they're looking for someone who isn't gunning for the big win. They want someone who is conservative, and who really understands the risks at hand. Someone who knows you have an advantage, you may not maintain it, so you had better take advantage of it while you can.

"Here at school we have a virtual stock exchange. A few months ago, we were each given five hundred thousand dollars of virtual money to play with. I've been playing the Internet stocks the entire time, but doing it on a very conservative basis. At three-thirty in the afternoon, I would look and see how NASDAQ and the Dow were doing along with thirty Internet stocks I was following. I would choose ones that were going in the same direction as the Dow. For example, if the Dow was up thirty points, I would take Amazon and eBay, if they were up, say, five points for the day. I would purchase them at three-thirty. I did this because I had noticed that between three-thirty and four, these stocks would jump through the roof because the individual investors will pop on-line at the end of the day and say, 'Oh, Amazon's up, I need to buy it.' And so the momentum pushes the stock up at the end of the day. But then more people would learn this news at night. They'd sit down, pick up the *Wall Street Journal* or watch the news, see that these stocks were up, and the following morning these stocks would skyrocket and then they'd come back right down. So what I would do is sell the stocks at market open. This way I had very little risk, but huge rewards. I turned five hundred thousand dollars into nineteen million dollars in four months. Partly, I was lucky. But to me, this was also a case of risk optimization. When the momentum was in my favor, I took advantage of it as quickly as I could—it was just like what I have learned to do in a sailboat race. If you've got the advantage, take it right now."

Tom Whidden of North Marine Group elaborates on

how the evaluation of risk affects the decision-making process. "To me, one of the biggest parallels that you can draw between business and sailing is the whole risk-to-reward concept. If you're in second place in a buoy race, and there's a twenty-boat-length gap to the leader, you would have to take a huge risk to try to win. Doing so could cost you a victory in the series—not just the individual race—so sometimes you need to realize second place is an acceptable outcome. In business, you have those kinds of situations all the time. If you had a chance to make ten thousand dollars more on a decision that puts the company at risk for five hundred thousand dollars—obviously you'd never do that."

Persistence Pays

If there are heroes among those employees who push the limits of an organization, their stories are usually ones of extraordinary perseverance and persistence against higher-ups or entrenched policies and systems that work to ensure the maintenance of the status quo. It often takes a fair amount of guts to buck the system in the first place. But to persist—even when you've been directed to no longer do so—takes an incredible amount of fortitude. During the course of developing the lightbulb, inventor Thomas Edison tried a thousand different materials for the bulb's filament. All failed. When asked if he felt that all this time was wasted, Edison replied, "Hardly. I have discovered a thousand things that don't work."

You might think that Roy Disney can get anything he wants at the Walt Disney Company; however, that's not really the case. Roy is a big believer in the power of the team and in developing a consensus that a new project is right for the company. For years, Roy has wanted to revive the studio's landmark film *Fantasia* as it was originally meant to be. Recently, he got his wish.

"My favorite picture of anything Walt had done was *Fantasia*. The original idea of *Fantasia* was that it would be a continual work in progress and we'd make new segments and add them in and take old ones out—it would be kind of a laboratory. Well, when Michael Eisner first came into the company and was quizzing me on my likes and dislikes, I told him that I wanted to update *Fantasia*. So, finally, when *Fantasia* went to video and sold huge, huge numbers of copies, I called Michael and said, 'You know what? Everybody loves the idea and, by the way, now we can afford it.' I've finally gotten to do it, and it was partly because I just kept saying, 'I want to do this and it's a good idea.' And it *is* a good idea. On January 1, 2000, we're coming out with *Fantasia 2000*—it's going to be released in every IMAX theater worldwide and run exclusively for four months. And it's virtually a brand-new picture. We've kept two of the original segments, and we've made seven new pieces with James Levine and the Chicago Symphony Orchestra—Kathleen Battle sings a little part of one of them. Walt used to call this "Stick-to-it-tivity.' A lot of successes I've had in life have been about being persistent. Persistence pays."

And persistence clearly paid when Roy saved the Disney Company from being dismantled and sold off in the eighties. While the Walt Disney Company has enjoyed a renaissance of creativity—not to mention financial success—over the past decade, this wasn't always the case. After Walt Disney died in 1966, and then his brother Roy—the company's financial genius—in 1971, the company began a financial death spiral that made it a tempting and easy target for the corporate raiders who were ready to break the company apart and sell it off piece by piece.

During this dark period in the company's history, Roy Disney—nephew of Walt, and son of Roy Sr.—made many suggestions to get the company back on track. For the most part, these suggestions were ignored by management. Says Disney, "I wanted to do something that was interesting and fun, and with them it was all about the sequel to *Herbie Goes to Monte Carlo*. And that's not fun."

Things got so bad that Roy left Disney in 1977 and, after watching the value of his stock plummet from $80 million to $45 million during the course of only six months, Roy resigned his position on the board of directors. For a man who not only had a very personal stake in the Disney legacy, and who had worked his way up in the organization—starting as an assistant film editor in 1954, and going on to produce more than forty television and theatrical productions for the company—cutting all ties with the organization was a particularly difficult decision.

But Roy had a plan.

Along with Stanley Gold, CEO of Shamrock Holdings, Roy's investment company, Disney barged his way back on to the board of directors in 1984—capturing three seats in the process. This gave Roy the power base he needed to bring in his own management team of Michael Eisner and Frank Wells. The rest, as they say, is history. With a new-found focus on animation—the heart and soul of the Walt Disney Company—one successful film after another was released to an enthusiastic movie-going public. First *The Little Mermaid*, which did $85 million in its theatrical release, followed by *Beauty and the Beast* ($160 million), *Aladdin* ($220 million), and *The Lion King* ($230 million).

Says Disney, "I think a lot of the successes I've had in my life have been about being persistent on things. When I quit the studio in '77, I just said, 'There are better places, but I think we can fix it someday.' And once a year we'd go visit somebody like Lehman Brothers and say, 'What do you think about proxy fights and what do you think about financing?' because the company was still making a profit. They were making a profit off what somebody before them had done, not what they were doing at that moment. Finally, in early '84, when things got really bad, we jumped in and, thanks to Stanley Gold, we were able to control it. So it's about staying power, I think more than anything else—staying with a good idea."

Ever since he first heard stories about the Transpac Race from Los Angeles to Honolulu, Roy has been enamored with it. And his quest to be on the first boat that crosses the finish line at Diamond Head Lighthouse is a story in persistence. In the late eighties, he built a sixty-eight-foot sled—a racing boat that specializes in the downwind sailing that is the hallmark of this passage—to win the race. This first *Pyewacket* was fast, but not fast enough to beat the brand-new—and growing—fleet of Bill Lee–designed Santa Cruz 70s that would dominate the West Coast ocean racing circuit for over a decade. After several years of frustrating racing—and a concerted effort on the part of Roy's crew to speed up the sixty-eight-footer, he decided to join the club and ordered the second *Pyewacket*, a Santa Cruz 70.

This new boat was quick, and very, very well sailed, garnering top honors in the highly competitive sled fleet in many of the long, offshore races down Baja California as well as the West Coast's series of round-the-buoys day races. Roy's trophy collection mounted, but his holy grail—line honors in the biannual Honolulu race—remained elusive no matter how close he came. One year, *Pyewacket* had a big lead on the fleet nearing the finish, only to sit wallowing for hours in a windless hole after the passage of a localized squall that cost its crew the race.

In 1995, the race rules changed, allowing bigger and faster boats. At that point, Roy made the commitment to "turbo-charge" his Santa Cruz 70, refitting the boat with a towering mast that supported a cloud of sail area plus a new keel fin with less drag. But that year in the Transpac, *Pyewacket* was beaten by another new turbo. So, Disney's team worked for two more years refining *Pyewacket*, setting numerous course records along the West Coast in the process. Everything was set for a full-on assault on the Transpac in 1997 when bad luck again struck. Roy suffered an injury in an auto accident a few months before the start. There was no way he could be on a boat in the middle of the ocean for nearly two weeks. But the team was prepped, and Roy sent the boat anyway—with his son Roy Pat in charge. As fate would have it, the conditions in the Pacific were the best in nearly two decades. *Pyewacket* not only was first to finish but she also set a course record in the process.

Roy was the biggest member of the cheering section when the boat arrived in Waikiki's Ala Wai harbor, but the fire still burned. Roy was back racing on his boat a few months later, and he had a plan for the next Transpac.

Rather than risk the chance that his decade-plus old design, albeit turbocharged, would be outclassed by newer boats, Roy decided it was time for *Pyewacket* number three. He hired the San Diego design firm of John Reichel and Jim Pugh to do an America's Cup–level analysis to come up with a design with a single purpose in mind—winning the Transpac. The new boat was launched in early 1999 and immediately won its first race—the eight-hundred-mile run from Florida to Montego Bay, Jamaica. On July 10, 1999, Roy Disney achieved his long-standing dream as he steered his new boat across the finish line off Diamond Head Lighthouse, shattering the old Transpac course record by three hours, forty-three minutes. His persistence paid off.

In order to pursue his love of sailboat racing, Tom Whidden made the switch from the nine-to-five rat race to become a sailmaker. It was not easy, especially when he and a partner, Peter Conrad, took over a small, Connecticut sail loft, Sobstad Sailmakers, that was best known for building sails for small boats for kids in the local area. But thanks to their talent, Tom and Peter put together a team that slowly grew the loft, expanding the product line to include bigger racing boats and Olympic classes. Still, Sobstad was a small fish in the big world of international racing. Nevertheless, Tom had his eye on the big prize—the America's Cup—and he dearly wanted to sell his sails to Dennis Conner. Tom's story of this quest is a perfect lesson in the power of persistence.

"I had followed the America's Cup since I was a kid. In 1978, I had been doing a lot of ocean racing and one guy I seemed to always come up against was Dennis Conner. So in late 1978, I called him up and I said, 'You know, I'd really like to be involved in your America's Cup campaign.' Dennis said sure, that would be okay with him. Then I told him, 'But I want to sell you sails.' 'Well,' Dennis said, 'my plan is to buy sails from North and Hood and, while I have a lot of respect for your sailing ability, I don't really have that much respect for your sails. You don't have any experience in the America's Cup so I just want to be honest with you—I'm going to stick with North and Hood.' So I said, okay, but keep me in mind when you are ready to try some of my sails."

Tom Whidden on Business, Dennis Conner, and the America's Cup

I immediately recognized that the America's Cup game, like most sailing, was just like business. You put a team together, you raise the money, and you did it early enough so that you had time to put your plan in place. There is the whole atmosphere of people getting along or not getting along and you have a finite amount of time to get the job done. You really don't get a profit and loss statement along the way, so it is a little different than business, a little different than school, where you get a report card. But you can tell how you are doing along the way and you can figure out how to go faster. I learned many lessons from Dennis Conner. I actually give him a lot of credit for my being as successful as I am in business and as successful as I am in sailing. He is good at both. What's funny about Dennis is that you can't pick just one thing that he is brilliant at, but you put them all together—he is brilliant. It was never his goal to be one hundred percent at every single thing or even at one thing necessarily. It was to be ninety percent at a lot of things. When you add up the whole thing it works pretty well.

"Later, in the 1979 SORC series in Florida, I raced a boat called *Love Machine* and Dennis sailed on a boat called *Williwaw*—we had some great battles. And after one of the races, Dennis came up to me and asked me where I was headed because he knew I was going to the airport. I said, 'I'm going home to Connecticut.' And he said, 'Great, I'll go with you.' I told Dennis that I was going to see my family and, while it would be nice to spend some time with him, I had some other things to do. Dennis said, 'Don't worry. I'll go with you anyway.' So he climbs on the plane with me to Hartford. He really should be going home to San Diego, but he climbs on the plane with me to go to Hartford and on the way up he asks me to join his America's Cup campaign. And I said, 'Well, you're going to have to buy my sails.' And he said, 'No, but you never know what'll happen.'

"So he finally talked me into it without a sail order, and I sailed with Dennis as his trial skipper in 1979 when he had the 12 Meters *Enterprise* and *Freedom* training one year before the 1980 America's Cup. And at the end of the summer, after I had done all this, I said, 'How about giving me a shot at the sails?' And he said, 'Okay, what do you want to build?' And I said, 'Well, honestly, I think I could do a good job on any of them but I don't think your spinnakers are very good.' So he said, 'Okay, well, let's try a spinnaker.' I said, 'okay.' I made him a spinnaker while he was away during a break period. We came back after the break and we tested it. And sure enough, it actually beat the other sails in tests. By the end of that campaign, it was North and Sobstad on Dennis's boats, not North and Hood."

Save a Little Horsepower

If you race sailboats for any length of time at all, you'll quickly learn that you don't need to blow everyone off the racecourse to win the race—you simply need to cross the finish line before anyone else. By calibrating your victories, you can save energy and resources—precious commodities for your next race.

As a result of his years of experience racing sailboats, Malin Burnham knows this lesson all too well. "We've still got to look at ourselves in the mirror, too. One can be overly competitive and be a complete ass about it. You can't just compete, compete, compete. There's got to be some balance in what you're trying to achieve. For instance, there's no reason to win by a lot. Save a little energy. Save a little dry powder for the next time—it'll come around. Next time always comes around. Another reason for that is that sometimes you don't want to be too noticeable to your competition. If they think you just got lucky and won that race by one boat length, even though you might have been able to win it by fifty boat lengths, then you don't become as much of a target. I think the same thing is true with business. You don't need to be way out ahead. You just need to be on top."

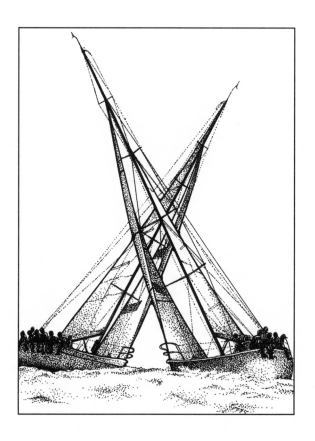

Chapter Nine

Rule Seven —
Master the Inner Game

I recently sailed on a seventy-foot sloop in a big weekend regatta in the waters of the Pacific Ocean off Los Angeles. On Saturday, we had one of those bad days. Our competition had been making improvements all year and on this day they dominated us. Not only that, but we were not sailing that well—our crew work was sloppy and overall concentration was down. As we returned to the dock on Saturday you could tell by body language that our team was down.

We had been the top boat for over a year, and we knew that we could do better—our experience told us that we had it in us. But when things are going badly, inertia often takes hold and the less committed person gives up trying so hard. But not that Sunday on our boat. That morning, on the way out to the racecourse, as the sea breeze built, we had a team meeting. We reminded ourselves that we could do better— that nobody was going to hand us the victory—and that just for the fun of it, we should sail the next two races with all the grit, determination, and teamwork we knew we had in us. We had done it before, it was a matter of digging deep and doing it again by letting the mental imagery of past peak performances raise our game.

It's an amazing feeling when you see such a turnaround in performance. We dug into our memory banks, put Saturday's poor performance out of our minds, and in its place envisioned what it was like in all those races that we had won. We ended the day with a first and a second and came back to the dock on top of the world. As it turned out our competitor beat us by just one point, but that did not matter—what mattered was that we had done our best.

Sometimes, the most difficult competition that we will ever face comes not from the companies, organizations, or markets that we constantly battle, but from ourselves. But once we are able to master ourselves—controlling the powerful emotions that often push us in the wrong direction, and harnessing the incredible energy within each one of us—*nothing* can stand in our way.

Attitude Is Everything

Think about the last time you hired a new employee. After you or your human resources department ran an advertisement in the newspaper for the position, you probably found yourself faced with one hundred or more résumés to look through in your spare time. What was it that separated one candidate from another in your mind?

You might have considered some of the following factors:

 * Experience in similar positions
 * Education and training
 * Organizations previously worked for
 * Longevity in each job

Each of these factors definitely has a role to play in the selection process—they can get a candidate's foot in the door, or relegate his or her résumé to the trash can. There is, however, one more thing that has a huge impact on the selection process, and it's something that can be very difficult to measure without meeting a candidate in person.

Attitude.

All the experience in the world can't buy you the right attitude. Neither can all of the education in the world, nor all of the connections you might have with suppliers, clients, or customers.

Simon Thomas, formerly National Sports Marketing Manager for Nike in Australia, and Commercial Manager of the 1993–94 Whitbread Around-the-World Race, currently works in the marketing and venue operations departments for the Sydney 2000 Olympic Games organizing committee. Early in his sailboat racing career, he made a mistake. From this he learned a very important lesson about commitment and attitude.

"There I was, as luck would have it, a member of New Zealand's first ever America's Cup challenge in Perth, 1986. A couple of weeks prior to the 12 Meter World Championships, I was training like a madman, the fittest and strongest I've ever been in my life, penciled in to be a pitman on one of New Zealand's first 12-Meter America's Cup boats. Except I didn't get picked! Not enough big-boat experience I was told—fair enough in hindsight [there were better guys around at the time] but as a gung-ho and very green twenty-two-year-old in his first attempt to crack into international big-boat sailing, I was mightily pissed off!

"Instead, I was offered the chance to be the 'twelfth man,' in essence, the boat boy. Part of the team, but not racing—responsible for maintenance and race preparation. Pumping hydraulic fluid from the bilges, longboarding the hull [sanding the hull of a boat with sandpaper glued to long boards of wood, a very arduous and dirty job], and long nights spent at the dock after everyone else had left for dinner, making sure everything was fixed for the next day.

"So what did I do? I said no! I'd just read *Born to Win*, John Bertrand's story of *Australia II*'s triumph in 1983 in Newport. In it he attributes his team's psychological edge to self-belief, in the guise of carefully cultured arrogance. That's me, I thought. I'm the best, and I'll prove it! I can run the foredeck better, tail halyards faster, grind harder and for longer. Not for me a backup role—the guy who hangs the shirts in the dressing room, and collects the laundry after the game. I won't be a lackey for anyone. I'll wait till I'm on the boat as a full-on racing crew—and then I'll prove I'm better than those guys!

"So what happened? The inevitable. One of the grinders got injured in the second race. And did I get the call as a replacement? Of course not. Did I deserve it? Of course not.

"Would I have gotten the call if I'd been the maintenance guy? Probably. Because, as I realized later, in this kind of team environment it's all about attitude. I had the wrong attitude. People recognize and reward the guy who doesn't complain, who works hard, who gets the dirty jobs done—even if he believes himself to be in the wrong place. To get ahead on a yachting team, you may not necessarily have to become a better sailor—perhaps you should become a better boat builder or engineer, or just plain better at scrubbing the bottom of a hull. And while these skills might be different from what you think you're best at—maybe that's where the team needs someone most. And, paradoxically, that's often the best way to get noticed, to get a break in the direction you really want to go.

"In business, there are menial tasks at every level. The key is to have patience and an eye for the big picture. Before you can demonstrate how great your skills are in one area, you will often have to show you have the right attitude in another area first. If you are acknowledged as a hard worker, then [and sometimes only then] do you get the chance to show how creative, innovative, and dynamic you are!

"When people reporting to me feel that a particular aspect of their job is beneath them, or they're bored, or they think they're in a rut [and most employees feel like this at some stage], this story becomes a useful motivational tool. I tell them of my America's Cup 'mistake,' and then I tell them to look honestly at themselves and get out and scrub the bottom of the boat. The good ones respond pretty well—and, if they do, there's usually a place on the crew for them before too long."

For Walt Disney Company vice chairman Roy Disney, the right attitude means an ability to have fun. "A big part of it for me is we laugh a lot. We keep a certain amount of perspective about how important all this really is to the bigger picture. If you blew something, fine, you blew something—now let's go and you can make up for it. But you've got to have fun. I've always said, 'The minute it's not fun, why should I do it?' Everybody seems to understand that. There are plenty of times to get serious."

And, sure, while winning races and setting records is a very enjoyable activity for Roy Disney, he fondly recalls lots of fun times on the water spent with family and friends. "When the kids were small, we had a Morgan 40 ketch. We'd throw the kids in the car, head down to Marina del Rey, and sail our boat to Catalina Island. I can remember one time in particular—it was evening, in the late spring. We got out about halfway across the channel to Catalina, and the sun was setting in a great big golden ball with a beautiful orange sun track shimmering across the water from the horizon to meet us. And on the other side of the sky, there was a full moon rising with a big silver track also meeting our boat. We had the big jib up and we were doing about seven knots. And our daughters who were probably eleven, twelve, thirteen, were sitting in the back of the cockpit with guitars, playing and singing 'Puff the Magic Dragon.' It doesn't get any better than that. Winning races is fun, too, but those magical moments on the water can't be equaled anywhere."

Back when I was racing dinghies in college, I hit a period where my teammate, Susan Daly, and I were in a slump. One evening after practice, an Olympic medalist named Glen Foster came to the Yale Corinthian Yacht Club to give a slide show about the Olympics. As I was listening I realized that here was this Olympian, a guy I had the ultimate respect for, and he was not talking about the fancy new sails he had developed for the Games, or how hard he and his crew had trained—he was talking about how much fun he had at the Olympics, living in the village and racing against tough competitors whom he respected. At that moment it dawned on me—Susan and I had gotten so focused on winning that we had lost the fun in our sailing.

So right then and there I made a promise to myself and to Susan that I would focus on getting the fun back into our racing. It didn't mean that we were any less serious. We just took the time to enjoy the racing and to take a look around and realize what a beautiful place the water is. And you know what? Our performance improved. We qualified for the Collegiate National Championships, and a few weeks later we won them! And it was all thanks to Glen Foster reminding me that performing at the ultimate level was still supposed to be fun.

Edsel B. Ford II, great-grandson of Ford Motor Company founder Henry Ford, and a director of the company, sums up attitude in three words: "Passion to win." Says

Ford, "I was fascinated with the competition of the America's Cup in Perth and the passion to win of the *Stars & Stripes* team. That same passion holds true with my cousin [Ford Motor Company chairman] Bill's and [Ford Motor Company president and CEO] Jacques Nasser's team. At Ford, we have this intense passion to succeed. And I think that, in the end, everybody wins. In sailing, when the boat wins, everybody wins including the crew, the designers, and the sponsors. At Ford, when we win, everybody wins including our customers, our employees, and our shareholders."

It's really true. If you *believe* you can accomplish something, and you commit your entire being to achieving your goal, then *nothing* will be able to get in your way. Once you have made your mind up, then your body will follow—not only will you *think* like a winner, but you'll *act* like one, too. And if you *act* like a winner, then you will *be* a winner.

For Tom Whidden, attitude is everything. "If you act like a winner, and you know you can win, then it's *easy* to win." He goes on to tell an anecdote from his team's unsuccessful defense of the America's Cup in 1983—the first time the Cup was lost in its 132-year history. "There's an interesting story from the 1983 America's Cup that illustrates my point perfectly. In that series, *Australia II* was *much* faster than our boat, *Liberty*—it was unbelievable. Yet, after four races, we were ahead 3–1. But you know what went wrong for us? The Australians won the next race, which was the fifth race of the series, a little bit by luck. That put them behind 3–2. Until then, we had them completely psyched out. But when they won that fifth race, all of a sudden the light came on in their heads that they were actually *faster* than us. Once the crew came to that realization—that they *could* win—then they started *acting* like it, and they won the Cup."

John Thomson, chairman of Thomson Industries, is an accomplished sailboat racer currently campaigning his Farr 40, *Solution*. He is well respected around the world as a rare "amateur" helmsman who can beat the pros—as he did steering his fifty-footer, *Infinity*, to an overall win in Hawaii's Kenwood Cup series in 1996. Thomson puts attitude at the top of his list of traits that are most important in both sailboat racing and business.

"If you think about it, attitude is one of the few things in life that you can control. On the racecourse, you can't control the wind, you can't control the tide, and you can't control what the other competitors do to you—the same as in business. In business you can't control what your competitors do to you, you can't control circumstances, and you can't control the general business environment. The one thing you *can* control is your attitude."

A few years ago I was giving a seminar with Dennis and some other top sailors, including the late Tom Blackaller. When queried on what the most important characteristic for a potential crew was, all the stars agreed: Attitude!

Racing with Ted Turner

Any time I get the chance to race with Ted Turner, I'll jump at it. I have sailed with Ted on both sides of the Atlantic and the Pacific, both before and after Turner Broadcasting hit the big, big time. Not only is he a great sailor—with an incredible amount of natural talent—but he is a charismatic leader on a boat and a heck of a lot of fun to have on board. Sure, he can get excited at times, but that's all part of his program—it shows how much he wants to win. Like the time we were sailing along in the English Channel in the Admirals Cup regatta. Ted was at the helm of our forty-three-foot boat, *Locura*, owned by George de Guardiola and Ricardo Vadia. It was the middle of the night, the second night of the race on one of those bone-chilling damp evenings where the dew began to fall at sunset and, even though it wasn't raining, you have your foul weather gear on. Everyone on deck is sleep-deprived—and wishing they could be down below tucked into a warm sleeping bag, or better yet, in a real bed at home.

All of a sudden, we spotted the white stern light of one of the competitors, one of the Italian boats. Ted started getting really excited as it was apparent that we were catching up. He began a constant stream of talking—exhorting every man on deck to concentrate on trimming the sails to take advantage of the slightest puff of wind. As we got closer, Ted kept getting more excited. It's then that the exhortations took a new tack—bribery!

"Come on, you guys—work hard here. Concentrate—we're catching them. Ease that spinnaker. If we pass these guys, I'll give everyone on deck ten thousand dollars! Come on—work hard!!!!!"

And after an hour of intense concentration, we passed the Italians. Nobody really expected Ted to pay up—that never happens in sailing—he was just trying to think of anything that would motivate the crew to get past that Italian boat. Winning was all that mattered at that moment.

But you know what? During that hour that Ted was driving—maintaining a running monologue throughout—none of us thought of how tired we were. We totally forgot about how cold our feet were in our damp sea boots. We were in the *Zone*! And Ted made it really fun!

Concentrate and Focus

The ability to concentrate and to focus on the task at hand is a skill that separates the best sailboat racers from those who always seem to end up at the rear of the pack. The best skippers—and the best managers—can turn their attention on like a laser, excluding any and all distractions from their view.

Tom Whidden remembers the historic race in the 1995 America's Cup Trials when Team Dennis Conner made a miracle come-from-behind move on the final leg of the race to pass the *America³* women's team to win the Defender Trials. "Their biggest problem was that they were too far ahead. It wasn't that they didn't know what they were doing. It wasn't even that they were complacent, although they might have been. It was that they were so far ahead it became difficult to cover their nearest competitor.

"I can tell you today how they could have done it better. They were four minutes ahead. They should have gone one way for two minutes and jibed over and gone the other way for two minutes and they would've been roughly between us and the next mark. But they probably figured they were so far ahead that they really didn't have to do that. And that's a little bit the same issue we have here at North Sails. We're very far ahead if we judge ourselves against our competitors, so we have to be very careful about becoming complacent. That's why we do things like strategic planning sessions, and that's why we have goals that we've set for ourselves that aren't just about profit and loss. They're things that measure how we think we're doing and whether we're continually making gains."

It can sometimes be very difficult to separate our emotions from our business dealings. Despite the trend toward automation taking over more and more of the day-to-day operation of many organizations, business is still very much a people thing, and people often allow emotion to color their decisions. To some degree, that's fine—we *are* all human, after all—but when emotion gets in the way of doing the right thing for our businesses, or when our personal feelings interfere with our ability to focus on executing the best decisions, then there is a very real problem.

This is a particularly important consideration for Elizabeth Meyer. "Don't be distracted by the people who are not your competition. Don't get into a luffing match with somebody who doesn't matter so that you end up in Timbuktu, and then look up ahead and go, 'Oh my God, there's the fleet!'

"It's easy to get mad at a particular person and think to yourself, 'I'm not going to let him catch up with me, and I don't care if I luff that person until I'm three miles behind.' You shouldn't do that on the racecourse or in business, even though the temptation is always there. I can personally get very distracted going for the finish if there's somebody that I really don't like in another boat. I can lose two places overall just to gain one place over somebody I'm mad at."

Victor Hadid, owner of Wilson Victor Associates, has seen firsthand what happens when sailors—and business-people—lose their focus and concentration, and allow emotion to take over. According to Hadid, "What happens with less experienced sailors is that they let their emotions take over and start screaming at the other boats. They'll start screaming, 'You fouled us! It's your fault.' Then the other boat will get caught up in it too and you'll see two full crews yelling at each other—back and forth. And you know what we do when that happens? We just sail right by them.

"We had a situation in Annapolis in the East Coast Championships last year. We were four days into the regatta and we were winning. We had a port-starboard situation and about sixteen or seventeen knots of breeze, four- to five-foot waves, and we're tacking in very, very, very tight quarters. In sailing, the general rule is that the starboard tack boat always has the right of way. However, there's a maneuver called lee-bow. What that means is that if you're on the starboard tack and I come up and I tack right underneath you, I can slow you down so it forces you to tack away. So, even though you're ahead of me, if I just come in and I get really close to you, I can suck the wind out of your sails and squirt through while kicking you to the back. I can turn your advantage to a disadvantage by tacking close to you.

"Our skipper hailed the other skipper and asked if he wanted us to tack or cross. It was very noisy and very windy, and our helmsman thought the other skipper responded by telling us keep sailing and cross ahead. But what the guy was really doing was waving his hand saying, 'No, no, no!' But you couldn't hear him; all you could do was look at the hand signal and it was ambiguous. So as we approached we prepared to cross him.

"It was nearly a major, major incident. There was no contact between the boats, but both boats ended up going head to wind and our sails were all over the place. Nobody fell into the water but both boats just erupted—*everyone* was upset. But on our boat, everybody was back in their positions quickly, we did a crash tack, and we were back to sailing. We had our boat completely back up to speed before they even had their sails trimmed back in on the other boat.

"That's a perfect example of how focus and concentration can make the difference between winning and losing. You're always going to be faced with crises, no matter how much you have prepared yourself in advance. But if everybody just refocuses on the goal, and concentrates their effort on getting the boat going again, you can make the best of a bad situation. By the way, we ended up coming in second in that race. [Author's note: There is a good chance Victor's boat committed a foul in this incident—if so, let's hope they did their penalty turns!]"

For John Bertrand, sailing teaches lessons that have value both in the world of sailboat racing, and in the world of business. "This sport does require solid organizational skills, and knowledge of technology, which is very much part of modern business, too. And then you have the need— the ability—to perform under extreme pressure. The inner game as well as the actual game is equally important if not more important when it really comes down to the wire, and all those elements are critical parts of day-to-day business.

So the world of sailing is interesting schooling for the world of business."

Relax, and Be Patient

Firefighting is a skill that every manager has to master as a matter of necessity. What would a typical workday be without at least one good crisis to have to deal with? One day it might be a hot new product introduced by your chief competitor, another day it might be an employee with an attitude problem. And on yet another day, your voice mail box—filled with all the messages you had meticulously saved while on the road—might self-combust.

It's no wonder we all get so caught up in jumping from one crisis to another—as the pace of business has increased over the past few decades, the number of problems has multiplied. Today, not only does it seem as if we have no choice but to fight the fires that flare up all around us, there is a certain satisfaction in successfully beating down another challenge.

Oftentimes, the best course of action is to refuse to get caught up in the latest crisis *du jour*, to instead slow down, step back, and take a look at the big picture. You'll be far more effective when you are calm than when you are overly excited. Tom Whidden of North Marine Group has this to say about the importance of relaxing when things get tough. "Whether I'm ahead or behind, my demeanor really doesn't change very much. I used to be a little bit more excitable but I would say that I've learned the hard way that that's not good leadership. In my experience, it's better not to show the crew an emotional difference between being ahead and being behind because, if the rest of the team sees that you're down when you're behind, or visibly up when you're ahead, it makes them mercurial, too. So I try really hard to be even-tempered. I'm not really sure what I've done to train myself to be like that. I mean, it's probably a little bit like being in a trance."

In some cases, being patient means adopting a strategy of waiting, and doing nothing. Says John Thomson of Thomson Industries, "I hear this all the time—both in sailing and in the business world: 'Let's do *something*. And I always say, 'No, no—you've got to understand that doing nothing *is* a strategy.' A lot of people lose sight of that. But sometimes you must hold your course and just wait to see what happens. The same thing happens in business. I see guys who say in response to some issue, 'We've got to do something.' And I say, 'Well, when you have a great idea, let's talk about it.'

"We had a situation when we were working a deal with a small company and things got quite emotional for the owner. I told our people to back off for a month or two. I said, 'If the deal goes away, it'll go away, but just be patient—we'll probably be successful in the long run.' Sure enough, the owner realized that what we were presenting was a good deal for him and he got over his emotional difficulties. We all kept a positive attitude and we worked it out; patience works.

"One of the things that I've learned on the racecourse from great sailors like Tom Whidden and Kenny Read is that you slow down and gain sometimes. One place where this really shows is at a mark rounding with a big pack of boats. You come in there, and your natural competitive tendency is to be aggressive, to stick your nose in and get the inside position. But that can be really risky. If you're not set up, and if your crew is not ready for this move, you will end up losing two or three boat lengths—or even risk a foul. It can be very painful to slow down and wait for a true opening, but I have seen it time and again—sometimes it pays to slow down. You gain because everyone *else* is making mistakes. Then you can be assured a good mark rounding with a clean hole and off you go. And I think that clearly applies to business."

Be Consistent

One of the things that most of us learn early on in our business careers is that we're expected to do a good job *every* day—not just every other day, or once a week, or once a month. Successful organizations depend on the consistent, high-quality performance of their workers to grow and to thrive. Inconsistent performance by workers begets inconsistent results—leading to poor-quality products and services. And these inevitably lead to disappointed customers and clients, who will quickly seek out companies that can deliver high-quality goods and services *consistently*.

Pete du Pont has learned a lot of lessons during the course of his varied career and his many hours on the water, but one of his most important lessons is that to be successful, you have to perform at a high level *consistently*. You don't always need to be number one—you just have to learn from your mistakes and then make fewer of them than your competition does.

Du Pont says, "Well, you certainly learn from catastrophic errors—if you get yourself in a port-starboard incident with another boat and have to do a 720-degree penalty turn, you'll remember that for quite a while. So the errors do teach you, but experience also teaches you not to get too excited. You learn, above all, to be consistent. You've got to look back over your history—either in business or sailing—and realize that to be successful, you've got to sail well a *lot* of times—not just this afternoon. And you've got to sell your products day in and day out. So, calm down and try to be consistent either in business or sailing.

"In sailing, it can take you a while to realize—particularly when you are young—not to bang the corners—a very high-risk strategy—just because it works once in a while. When it works, it feels great. But if you keep on trying it you'll find yourself in the back of the fleet more often than at the front. At some point, you need to realize that's a mistake. It's better to employ more conservative tactics that keep you closer to the fleet where you can let other things like boat speed and good crew work come to play rather than hang it all out on a high-risk, make-or-break maneuver.

"In my political career, I did an awful lot of debating with other candidates. And when you're debating, consistency is really important because the people in the audience have a variety of interests. What they want to hear from you is that you've got some sensible ideas on a variety of subjects, because one listener will be interested in education, and somebody else in taxes, and somebody else in retirement, and somebody else in global warming. And if you have three good positions and one screwball one, the people think 'Gee, he was pretty good until he got into taxes.' If you're inconsistent, you might get lucky once in a while, but in the long run it's not going to work."

As editor of IntellectualCapital.com, an Internet-based weekly public-policy e-zine, du Pont is constantly experiencing the demands—and the rewards—of producing a high-quality product *consistently*. In the limited attention span of many Net surfers, to do anything less is a recipe for an instantaneous loss of readership—along with the resulting drop in page views, banner ad click-throughs, and advertising revenue.

Says du Pont, "I'm in the business now of producing Internet publications, and every Thursday we have to publish a magazine with twenty original articles in it. The challenge with a publication is that you've got to be interesting or people aren't going to read it. But, with a twenty-article magazine, you've got to have consistent quality. Our biggest challenge is finding really interesting pieces of consistently good quality each and every week."

George David, chairman and CEO of United Technologies, believes in the value of consistency. "I like to quote Deming's [W. Edwards Deming, the American quality expert credited with launching the Japanese quality revolution of the 1970's and later] fourteenth principle: constancy of purpose. You get good products and a good company and a good sailing program out of consistency, out of 'constancy of purpose.' It takes a long time to do good things in life. You need to be good at what you do, but you also need to do most things for a while to be good at them. You don't typically find somebody with a brand new racing program winning in five seconds flat. The same is true in business.

"Along with consistency, you need predictability. And about the best way I get predictability with people is to rely on their principles. When people have principles, when they have beliefs, and you know these, you will almost always know where they will be on an issue. I like that relationship between beliefs and outcomes, and it's a really key part of choosing your closest associates. Principled people are predictable, and when you turn the idea around, it's also true: Unpredictable people are unprincipled. Nobody wants unprincipled people anywhere near them. And it's true in sailboats just as it is in business."

Business student Drew Freides agrees. He says, "The most important thing is it has to be consistent throughout a racing campaign or you won't win. In business, you have to be consistent with your employees—from hiring them, to training them, to motivating them. Consistency starts from the top of the organization, making sure that everyone in the organization is clear that this is our goal, this is how we want to go about doing it, this is what it's going to take, and this is what we're asking you to do. So if some people aren't interested in the organization's direction, or if they just don't fit, then it can get sorted out early on. If an employee's goals no longer fit with those of the company, then you can either try to bring them back together, or move your separate ways."

For Bill Koch, consistency is one of the key determinants of success. It's not a matter of raw intelligence, it's a matter of doing the right thing more often than your competition does. "The team that wins is the one that makes the least mistakes, not the one that is the most brilliant. Ted Turner once told me, 'I don't care about technology. I'll just get on a boat and I'll out-sail the other guy.' It's all about making no mistakes."

When I was in college, we had a great team at Yale including Steve Benjamin and Dave Perry—two guys who have continued to have a major impact in the sport of sailing. Intercollegiate racing is intense—you race every weekend spring and fall season. Collegiate dinghy sailing is formatted so that the races are really short—on the order of about twenty minutes—so with two fleets of boats going, a regatta could easily have more than twenty races in just one day. The boats are identical—supplied by the host club—and you rotate into a new boat regularly, so there is no way to gain an advantage with a faster boat; needless to say, with all those races, the emphasis is on consistency. At the college nationals—the culmination of the racing season—a team that averages fifth-place finishes in a field of fifteen will almost always win. Of course there is nothing like the feeling of winning a race—"getting a bullet"—but in college sailing it rarely pays to take the higher-risk course that might result in an outright win. It's much better to use good, conservative tactics and plug away. Steve Benjamin used to repeat a saying that famed Long Island sailor, Jim Miller, would say: "I'm the garbageman. I'll get those seconds, thirds, and fourths—then win the regatta. Yep, I'm the garbageman!"

Learn from Your Mistakes

We all make mistakes at work; however, we all don't *learn* from our mistakes. Most managers can excuse an employee's mistakes—especially if they are as a result of trying to innovate or take initiative on behalf of the organization or its customers—what managers cannot excuse, however, is the employee who repeats the same mistake over and over again, ignoring the lessons that the mistake can teach.

Marilyn Wilson-Hadid, vice president of strategic planning and new business development for Fisher-Price, believes that it is important for a team—win or lose—to review their performance after a race. This also holds true in business, where employee teams should spend time after completing a project to review the things that went well, and the things that didn't go so well. The point is to bring everything out into the open and to learn from successes (so you can do more of that the next time), as well as failures (so you can do fewer of those).

According to Wilson-Hadid, "It's the whole idea of a learning organization. A really good crew is self-critical in a positive way. At the end of the day, they'll sit around and revisit the tack that they missed, or a foul during a mark rounding that caused them to have to go back, or the time when they knew the competition was going to the right side of the course and they should have followed them, but they didn't. The benefit of this is that when they hit the same kind of situation again, they're armed with a knowledge of how to handle it instead of giving up and saying, okay, it's the end of the race—let's go have a beer and not worry about it, which a lot of people do. There's nothing wrong with that, but you're losing an opportunity to learn valuable lessons."

America's Cup winner Bill Koch goes to great lengths to learn from his own mistakes, and to facilitate learning among the members of his teams. In one case in particular, a momentary lapse of attention between Koch and another member of his crew cost Koch the race, as well as a very expensive piece of hardware. "At one of the Maxi World Championships, we were rounding the last mark—heading toward the finish line. One guy was working the hydraulics and I was working the winch. The guy who was working the hydraulics switched it on to the checkstay and, unfortunately, I was grinding up the runner. So as we rounded the last mark, we broke the mast.

"I put that mast up as a flagpole in my marina at the Cape as a reminder of what one mistake can do to you. After that, we built a working model of the mast—with all the control lines on it: the backstay, headstay, checkstay, runners, and so on—and let people play with it so you could see what would really happen to a mast if you put too much tension in one area and not enough in another. And then we redesigned the hydraulic system on the Maxi so you couldn't make that mistake again."

And anyone in an organization—from the most experienced, to the least—can always learn something new. When the stars in an organization show their colleagues that they are not too proud to admit their mistakes and learn from them, the effect on an organization can be profound. Koch continues, "During the 1992 America's Cup competition, we lost the second race to the Italians, so I organized a review of the mistakes that we had all made in that race. I also organized a 'Come to Jesus' session with the crew. I had the coaches prepare by studying the films to make very good diagrams of what went wrong. I got into the crew meeting the next day and Buddy Melges [Koch's primary helmsman] said he couldn't sleep that night, and that he wanted to go over a few things. And I said, 'Well, Buddy, I've arranged this whole presentation. Let's go over your things afterward.' But he persisted. Buddy and I butted heads for about ten minutes on what this meeting was going to be. Finally I said, 'Okay, Buddy, what do you have?' And he had made a list of twenty-eight mistakes, of which he personally made twenty. So I said, 'Okay, Buddy, it's your meeting!'

"He took the attitude that he made mistakes—and everybody made mistakes—but we've got to correct these mistakes if we're going to win. And I think that was a terrific example of what people can do if they have the right attitude and if they learn from their mistakes. If a guy like Buddy Melges—a guy who's won an Olympic Gold Medal and a host of world championships, a guy considered to be one of the best sailors in the world—if he could put his ego below the ego of the boat, we could go out and surmount any problem. And we did—we won the Cup. The fact that our team—a relatively inexperienced crew by Cup standards—could go out and compete with the very best in the world and win, that shows you what you could do in *any* field if you have the right attitude, the right focus, and the right sense of teamwork. Ordinary people can do extraordinary things if they work together as a team with focus, attitude, and teamwork."

Of course, when you learn something new, it doesn't have to be as a result of a mistake, it can be because of changes in your business environments, or your markets, or your competition. You may be forced to learn new tricks in order to survive. Business student and sailor Will Graves has noticed a big change in the environment of both sailboat racing and business. Where in the past, people tended to specialize in narrow tasks or bands of expertise, today they are required to learn a much broader range of skills to be successful. Says Graves, "This whole thing is what we call intermediation. It's the changing of the economy where the middleman is going away and people are increasingly dealing directly with producers. Sailing is moving that way, too. It seems you have to be a bit more well rounded nowadays. In the past, for example, in an offshore race, you would just get a weather report from the weather service every six hours. Now there is technology to actually get weather charts and satellite images on the boat and look at them out on the water—you have to be able to interpret the information yourself.

"The whole Internet economy is removing the middleman. Companies are increasingly going directly to the consumer—using the Internet they can do that. For instance, if you want to buy a computer, you don't have to go to a store. Today you can visit the Dell Computer Web site and create your own custom machine out of hundreds of different choices of features and equipment. You don't have to go to some place like Circuit City or CompUSA and have the salesperson tell you what he or she *thinks* you really want."

To say that John Thomson, chairman of Thomson Industries, is a true believer in the power of the lessons that sailboat racing can teach would be an understatement. He is so committed to this belief that he has arranged for many of his employees and managers to take sailboat lessons on their own time and to participate on the water in some spirited racing. The lessons in teamwork that they learn help to reinforce the company's own teamwork workshops and other training activities.

Says Thomson, "We borrowed a couple of Sonar sailboats and picked some of my senior executives—none of whom knew how to sail—and told them to show up one Friday in the morning with T-shirts, jeans, sneakers, and a jacket. We said that we had a business assignment for them. Then I brought them down to the marina, gave them about a half an hour indoctrination and about an hour on the boat, and said, 'There are no direct reports here. You're going to go out there and sail, do a match race series.'

"We had some observers on each boat to keep them out of trouble, but they let my staff try to figure out everything for themselves. They were all fouled up the first couple of races, and one was real late to the start but the last race was really, really close and they had a lot of fun. It was a great demonstration of what teamwork could do. The event was so successful that we're starting a sailing class within the company to teach people who are interested—on their own time, after hours—to sail and to learn the fundamentals of racing and teamwork."

Howie Hamlin on Sailing and
Business Success

Howie Hamlin is a residential land broker for Whittlesey Doyle. Hamlin specializes in selling expensive pieces of land to home builders. He is also an expert dinghy racer, a long-time stalwart of the 505 class—a seventeen-foot ultra-high-performance racing dinghy that features some of the most competitive international racing around. Over the past three years, this hardworking businessman has also achieved a remarkable record at the class's highest level. With incredibly consistent finishes of one, two, three, two at the last four annual 505 World Championships, he and his crew Mike Martin are number one in the class's worldwide ranking system.

Twenty-five years racing in the class is one of Howie's secrets to success, but as his time commitment to business has increased, his sailing time has taken a sharp dive. Interestingly, his results do not reflect this—in fact, they have improved. Why? Because of Hamlin's methodical system for reviewing his boat's weaknesses and improving its strengths.

Says Hamlin, "In our 505 campaign, time management is absolutely critical. There are precious few weekends available for training, so we train on the weekday evenings when daylight savings time kicks in. We start by focusing on our weaknesses. And those come out of my extensive notes from the last event. It's like in business where you look back and say, 'Where did we go wrong last year? What were our deficiencies? What areas do we need to improve?' We do the exact same thing in sailing. This year we had two goals: to improve our upwind speed in really windy conditions, and improve our downwind speed in light air. And that's only two out of probably twenty different areas that we could have looked at, but, given the time available, we set strict priorities so we would not be distracted.

"For upwind sailing, we focused on centerboard blade development. This was an area that had not been looked into in over a decade. We started playing with different shapes—profiles and flexibility—and discovered some pretty significant speed gains. For downwind sailing, we thought that our problem was either sail trim or technique and it turned out that we simply weren't pulling the centerboard up all the way. We had always kept it down three inches, but by pulling it up all the way out of the water, we went from being slow to being incredibly fast. It was so simple, the easiest thing to do. It took no effort, no work on our part. I've been sailing the boats for twenty-five years and that's all it was!"

Epilogue

Rules to Race By

As I write this Epilogue, I'm in Auckland, New Zealand, practicing with Team Dennis Conner for my third America's Cup on board *Stars & Stripes*. But although we're working as hard as we possibly can—from dawn's first light until well after dark—to get ready for our first races against the other challengers, I am again reminded of the lessons that led me to write this book in the first place.

On Thursday Dennis Conner was at the helm as we towed our beautiful 75-foot America's Cup boat out in the late morning; there was not a breath of wind on the Hauraki Gulf. So he called over to our tender (the big motorboat that was towing us) and asked his good friend, local sailing legend Murray Ross, to recommend a good place for lunch. Murray suggested a restaurant on a nearby island,

and the plan was forged. We towed at fourteen knots through some of the most beautiful scenery I have ever seen: rocky island shores, rolling green pastures, and pine tree forests. Auckland's waterfront is a virtual archipelago of islands.

After an hour and a half—during which time D.C. entertained the crew with old sailing "war stories"—we pulled alongside our tender as it dropped the hook on a beautiful mile-long sandy beach. Needless to say, the locals were astounded—an America's Cup boat had never before come within two hundred yards of the beach and dropped anchor (we were twenty miles from the Hauraki Gulf race course by now). We took the inflatable support boat into wading distance of the beach, rolled up our pants, and jumped into the water, heading for the beach. Soon we were being catered to in a local island restaurant/pub while the locals looked over their beer mugs at the strangest crowd they had ever seen. An hour or so later we headed back to the boats. The sea breeze was just coming in, so we hoisted the sails and headed for home—an idyllic day in the life of the America's Cup.

The entire adventure was engineered by Dennis Conner as a special treat for the guys who he is counting on to help him win his fifth America's Cup. When he saw that there was no wind, instead of having the boat towed back to the base for an afternoon of work, or waiting for hours for the breeze to come up—as any other team would have done—Dennis did something different. For a few hours, he took us far away from the nonstop intensity of America's Cup competition and helped us all to remember why we were here in the first place: for the love of sailing. Not only did he demonstrate what true leadership is all about, but he forged strong bonds with each and every one of us that afternoon— bonds that will only get stronger as competition progresses.

The message is clear: *People* are an organization's most important asset. Successful organizations today depend on a talented and motivated workforce to pull ahead of the competition and to stay out in front. And as Dennis so amply demonstrated on that warm and sunny day, true leadership is knowing when to work hard, and when to stop and smell the roses. It's knowing how to reward your employees for doing a good job, and it's knowing how to build a team that can overcome *any* challenge. And together, I have no doubt in my mind that we will.

Biographies

Kurt Antonius is senior manager of public relations for American Honda Motor Company, Inc., in Torrance, California. The Acura Division of American Honda Motor Company is sponsor of the annual Acura SORC (Southern Ocean Racing Conference) regatta, held since 1938 in South Florida, and attracting a fleet of more than two hundred boats from around the country and abroad.

John Bertrand is Australia's best-known sailor. The first non-American skipper to win the America's Cup, Bertrand and his crew aboard the wing-keeled *Australia II* broke America's 132-year winning streak by beating Dennis Conner's *Liberty* four races to three to win the Cup in 1983. Bertrand is an Olympic Bronze medalist in the one-person Finn class. He returned to the America's Cup game in 1995 with his *oneAustralia* campaign that was runner-up in the trials to the victorious Kiwis. Bertrand is vice chairman and cofounder of Quokka Sports, an on-line provider of digital sports entertainment.

Dean Brenner is a financial adviser for PaineWebber, Inc, in Hartford, Connecticut. As the member of a five-person money management team, Brenner is responsible for managing $650 million of personal assets. Brenner is a crew in the Olympic Soling class for Tony Rey. Currently they are the number-one–ranked American Soling team.

Malin Burnham is chairman of the board of John Burnham & Company, an insurance and commercial real estate broker based in San Diego, California. In 1945—at age seventeen—Malin became the youngest sailor ever to win the Star World Championships. Burnham was responsible for organizing the San Diego Yacht Club's successful 1987 America's Cup Challenge in Perth, Australia, and he has skippered or crewed in countless races all around the world.

Dennis Conner is arguably the most successful sailboat racer in history. He has won dozens of world championships in a variety of classes, the America's Cup four times, three times as helmsman, and a host of other major events. In 1987, Conner made the cover of *Sports Illustrated* and *Time* magazine in the same week for winning back the America's Cup from Australia. He is currently mounting a campaign to win back the Cup again, this time from New Zealand.

George David is chairman and CEO of $26 billion United Technologies Corporation of Hartford, Connecticut. He has campaigned a series of Long Island Sound–based boats named *Idler*. The most recent *Idler*, a fifty-footer, was launched in late 1998 and was part of the U.S. team in the 1999 Admiral's Cup.

Norwood Davis is chairman of the board and CEO of Trigon Healthcare, Inc.—the largest health care insurance company in Virginia—headquartered in Richmond, Virginia. The company has four thousand employees and serves more than 1.8 million customers through a variety of regional and statewide networks. Norwood Davis is also an avid sailboat racer, keeping the competition on its toes at the helm of his boat *Prima*.

Richard (Dick) DeVos is president and co-CEO of Amway Corporation, based in Ada, Michigan. With more than $5.6 billion in sales, fourteen thousand employees, and 3 million independent distributors worldwide, Amway is the largest direct-sales company in the world. DeVos has owned a series of racing boats named *Windquest* that have won most of the Midwest's major races and many more around the world. He currently campaigns a One Design 48 on the grand-prix circuit around the United States.

Roy E. Disney is vice chairman of the Walt Disney Company. Roy is a longtime sailor. He has owned a series of lightweight racing sloops named *Pyewacket*—after a cat belonging to a witch in John Van Druten's play *Bell, Book, and Candle*—that hold most of the long distance records on the West Coast including several different races to Hawaii. His latest *Pyewacket*, a seventy-two-foot-long "turbo-sled," was launched in early 1999 and was first to finish and set a new course record in the 1999 Transpacific Yacht Race to Honolulu.

Pete du Pont is the editor of IntellectualCapital.com, a weekly on-line public policy journal. Du Pont has served as a Delaware state legislator, U.S. congressman, and governor, and in 1988 was a Republican candidate for President of the United States. He is a director in the Wilmington, Delaware, law firm of Richards, Layton & Finger and an accomplished sailor. Recently he's been campaigning a One Design 35 with great success, including a victory at the prestigious Key West Race Week in 1999.

Jay Ecklund is former chairman of Minnesota-based Young America Corporation, a rebate-and-coupon fulfillment business. Ecklund, who sold Young America to BT Capital Partners in 1997, actively (and very successfully) campaigns his One Design 48 racing yacht *Starlight* at a variety of high-profile regattas throughout the year. Ecklund's boat was first in class at the 1999 SORC and won the Governor's Trophy for posting the best results for a PHRF entry.

Chris Ericksen is sales manager at Allied Pacific Metal Stamping in Anaheim, California. He races Etchells class sailboats whenever he gets the chance.

Edsel B. Ford II is a member of the Board of Directors of Ford Motor Company and its Finance Committee. He is chairman of the company's Centennial Committee, and the company's primary liaison with the National Automobile

Dealers Association. Ford is a director of Penske Motor-sports, Inc., and was formerly president and chief operating officer of Ford Motor Credit Company. He was involved in Ford's sponsorship of Dennis Conner's winning *Stars & Stripes* America's Cup campaign in 1987.

Drew Freides is a student at the Darden Graduate School of Business Administration of the University of Virginia in Charlottesville and served as a summer associate in the Equities Division of Goldman, Sachs & Company. He was captain of the varsity sailing team, and worked for eight years at Nelson/Marek Yacht Design—one of the world's leading designers of racing sailboats. In 1995 Drew managed the construction of the 1995 America's Cup yacht *Young America*. He has sailed on behalf of the United States in many international regattas and ocean races.

William (Will) B. Graves is currently pursuing his MBA at The Wharton School at the University of Pennsylvania in Philadelphia. Graves is a graduate of the U.S. Naval Academy and worked as an information technology and business process reengineering consultant for Deloitte and Touche LLP and for the U.S. Navy as a Surface Warfare Officer. He managed an Olympic Star Class sailing campaign in 1996, was a member of Team Dennis Conner's 1995 America's Cup Defense, and was a member of the 1991 and 1992 Collegiate National Sailing Champion team and was named First Team All-American.

Victor Hadid is owner of Wilson Victor Associates and WOW (Wild Opportunities Worldwide), an import-export firm that sells to national retailers such as Wal Mart, Target, and others. With his wife Marilyn, he sailed on David Brodsky's Swann 57 during the 1999 Block Island Race Week (along with Dennis Conner) and is campaigning an IMX38 toward the LORC championships. Victor also is a bowman for Geoff Moore, 1999 J-24 North American champion.

Howie Hamlin is a residential land broker and partner with Whittlesey Doyle, specializing in selling large pieces of land. Hamlin is the 1999 505 Class World Champion, and four-time (1990, 1992, 1996, and 1999) 505 Class North American Champion.

Kelvin Harrap is an America's Cup and Whitbread Around the World Race veteran from New Zealand. He sailed the 1997–98 Whitbread on Dennis Conner's *Toshiba*.

Robert Hughes is owner of Advantage Benefits Group (ABG) in Grand Rapids, Michigan. ABG structures employee benefit plans (401k, pension, health, cafeteria, life, and disability) for employers throughout the Midwest. Hughes owns a One Design 35 and Melges 24 (*Heartbreaker*) and has sailed competitively since 1986.

Gary Jobson is a world-class sailor, television commentator, author, and corporate adviser based in Annapolis, Maryland. Jobson won the America's Cup, serving as tactician for Ted Turner in 1977, the 1979 Fastnet Race, and many of the world's ocean races. In college he was named an All-American sailor three times and was twice named College Sailor of the Year (1972, 1973). Jobson has been ESPN's sailing commentator since 1985 and is an editor-at-large for *Sailing World* and *Cruising World* magazines.

Bill Koch appeared on the sailboat racing scene in the 1980s owning a series of highly successful maxi-boats named *Matador*. An amateur sailor, Koch rocked the world of racing by mounting an effort to win the America's Cup in 1992 and doing it! His *America³* campaign was founded on "talent, teamwork and technology." For the subsequent Cup campaign, Koch's organization sponsored the first ever all-women's team to race for the America's Cup. Bill Koch is founder and president of Oxbow Corporation in West Palm Beach, Florida, a firm specializing in alternative energy, coal, oil, composite pipe, and real estate.

Mark Landwer is vice president of national accounts for Hartford Computer Group, Inc. (HCG), of Inverness, Illinois. HCG has annual sales of approximately $500 million with 425 employees in seventeen locations nationwide. Landwer enjoys racing his Farr 40 on Lake Michigan.

Elizabeth Meyer performed a yacht restoration miracle by devoting five years of her life to the inch-by-inch rebuild of T.O.M Sopwith's 1934 America's Cup challenger, the J-boat *Endeavour*. She is the founder and CEO of the International Yacht Restoration School in Newport, Rhode Island, and is president of J-Class Management, which manages the operation and chartering of several classic yachts, including the J-boats *Endeavour* and *Shamrock V*.

Ben Mitchell was vice president and general counsel for Logicon for more than eighteen years. An All-American sailor at USC, and highly ranked Star Class skipper, Benny inherited a love of sailing from his late father, legendary navigator Ben Mitchell, Sr. He is a longtime crew member for both Jack Woodhull and Roy Disney.

Ross Ritto is CEO of Southern California Sound Image, Inc., in Escondido, California. Ritto combined his love for sailboat racing and business to design and patent a revolutionary speaker enclosure using carbon fiber technology. Ritto's company has produced shows and tours for many musical acts including Jimmy Buffett, Mary-Chapin Carpenter, Barbara Mandrell, Crosby, Stills, and Nash, Melissa Etheridge, and many others. Ritto regularly races his Farr 40 *High Five* to great success on the West Coast.

Chuck Robinson is president of DynaYacht, a hi-tech sailboat design company. A former Deputy Secretary of State under Gerald Ford, he is a longtime Nike board member and chairman of Nike's finance committee. Chuck recently retired from the board of Northrop and has over forty years of successful business experience in mining and ocean transportation.

Alex Sozonoff is vice president of customer advocacy for Hewlett-Packard Company. He is responsible for raising H-P's overall skill set in the area of relationship management with the Computer Organization's key enterprise accounts and selected strategic partners. Sozonoff was previously responsible for managing the company's sponsorship of World Cup soccer, Formula One auto racing, and America's Cup sailing teams. In 1997, Sozonoff was named Executive of the Year by the National Account Management Association.

Mike Spence is former dean and Philip H. Knight Professor of Economics and Management at Stanford University's Graduate School of Business. Spence holds the John Bates Clark Medal, given biennially to a person under the age of forty who has made a "significant contribution to economic thought and knowledge." Immediately before coming to Stanford, Spence served as dean of the Faculty of Art and Sciences at Harvard. Whenever he gets the time, Spence loves to windsurf in San Francisco Bay.

J. Douglas (Doug) Stewart is CEO of TechTouch Systems in Santa Fe, New Mexico, and an organizational consultant, author (*The Power of People Skills*), and public speaker. Dr. Stewart is also a performance consultant to the Boston Red Sox baseball organization and an instructional consultant to Steve and Doris Colgate's Offshore Sailing School. His sailing team won the 1997 Sailmaker's Caribbean Challenge regatta in the British Virgin Islands.

Simon Thomas was National Sports Marketing Manager for Nike in Australia, and Commercial Manager of the 1993–94 Whitbread Around the World Race. Simon currently works in the marketing and venue operations departments for the Sydney 2000 Olympic Games organizing committee. Prior to getting a "real job," Simon was an active racer, and even crewed for Peter Isler once in an Auckland match race regatta.

John Thomson is chairman of Thomson Industries, Inc., of Port Washington, New York, and one of the most successful amateur helmsmen in the world of yacht racing. Over the past two decades, John has owned a series of forty- to fifty-foot racing sailboats and amassed an enviable record including first overall at the 1996 Kenwood Cup, besting a fleet of professional helmsmen. Currently, John campaigns his Farr 40 *Solution* and his winning ways have continued in this highly competitive class.

R. E. (Ted) Turner is vice chairman of Time Warner, Inc., overseeing many of the company's entertainment assets including Turner Broadcasting System, Inc. (TBS), Cable News Network (CNN), Home Box Office, Inc. (HBO), Cinemax, and the Atlanta Braves and Atlanta Hawks professional sports franchises. Turner won the America's Cup in 1977 at the helm of *Courageous*, the 1979 Fastnet Trophy aboard his sixty-eight-foot sloop *Tenacious*, and four Rolex Yachtsman of the Year awards.

Dick Watts is president and CEO of ConvergeNet Technologies, Inc., a provider of enterprise data storage solutions in San Jose, California. Prior to joining ConvergeNet, Watts had a successful thirty-year career at Hewlett-Packard, where he managed several multibillion-dollar global businesses and since 1992 served as corporate vice president. His last position at Hewlett-Packard was general manager of the

Computer Sales and Distribution Group, where he directed the worldwide sales forces for all of H-P's computer systems, PCs, printers, and services. Watts is an avid sailor, campaigning a J-105-class sailboat on San Francisco Bay. Watts's team was the season champion in 1998.

Tom Whidden is president of North Marine Group, parent company of North Sails, the largest and most successful manufacturer of performance sails in the world. Tom has sailed in the America's Cup five times, winning it three times—always with Dennis Conner. Tom is to blame for Peter Isler's involvement in the America's Cup, too.

Marilyn Wilson-Hadid is vice president of strategic planning and new business development for toymaker Fisher-Price in East Aurora, New York. With her husband Victor, she sailed on David Brodsky's Swann 57 during the 1999 Block Island Race Week (along with Dennis Conner) and is campaigning an IMX38 toward the LORC championships.

Jack Woodhull is former chairman and CEO of Logicon, Inc., a company focused on delivering advanced technology and information systems and services to a variety of government agencies and scores of commercial enterprises.

Glossary of Sailing Terms

aft: Toward the rear of a boat.

B-maxer: An endearing term for a very large crew member whose most important job is sitting at the boat's widest point—the B-max—to counteract the forces of the wind.

boom: The horizontal pole that supports the bottom edge of the mainsail.

bow: The front of a boat.

bowman/bowperson: The crew member assigned to work at the front of the boat, managing the setting and dropping of headsails.

buoy: A floating object that can be used as a turning mark in a race. Anchored so that it does not float away.

buoy race: A race sailed around a series of buoys. Usually an hour or two in duration.

close-hauled: The closest course to the wind that you can effectively sail upwind. Also called sailing "upwind," "on the wind," or "beating."

cockpit: The area where the crew operates the boat, usually in the middle or rear part of the boat.

deck: The top of the hull.

dinghy: A sailboat, usually under twenty feet in length, with a centerboard (or daggerboard or leeboard) instead of a ballasted fixed keel fin found on a keel boat.

downwind: (1) Sailing with the wind coming from behind you. (2) Also, the direction that the wind is blowing toward.

fleet race: A race in which many boats compete together.

halyard: The rope running up the mast used to pull a sail up.

headsail: Any sail hoisted forward of the mainsail.

heel: When the boat leans to one side.

helm: (1) The wheel or tiller—the device used to steer a boat. (2) The position of the helmsman on the boat.

helmsman/helmsperson: The driver or skipper of the boat.

hike: To lean your body out over the side of a boat, usually to counteract the heeling forces on a dinghy.

hoist: To pull sails up the mast.

hull: The body of the boat.

jib: The most common headsail.

jibe: To change a boat's direction of travel by turning away from the wind until the wind is blowing upon the opposite side of the boat. Also commonly spelled *gybe*.

keel: A fixed, ballasted center fin that keeps the boat from sideslipping while providing stability to prevent capsizing or tipping over.

layline: The line beyond which you can lay (make) the destination on a close-hauled course with no more tacks.

leeward: Downwind; away from the wind.

mainsail: The sail farthest to the rear of a boat with one mast, normally attached to the mast along its front edge.

mainsheet: The rope that pulls the boom (and hence the mainsail) in and out.

mast: The vertical pole that supports the sails.

match race: A race between only two boats.

multihull: A boat with multiple hulls such as a catamaran or trimaran.

port: Left.

port tack: Sailing with the wind coming over the left side of the boat.

puff: An increase in wind velocity.

regatta: A series of races scored as a whole.

rig: The mast and standing rigging; also a term for preparing the boat (or sail or fitting) for use.

rudder: The underwater fin that steers a boat; controlled by a tiller or wheel on deck.

sloop: A common rig with one mast supporting a mainsail and jib.

spinnaker: A big, colorful, parachute-like specialty sail used when sailing downwind.

starboard: Right.

starboard tack: Sailing with the wind coming over the boat's right side.

stern: The back end of the boat.

tack: (1) To change a boat's direction of travel by turning toward the wind, beginning with the wind blowing on one side and ending with it blowing on the other. (2) The boat's heading in relation to the wind (that is, on *starboard* or *port tack*).

trapeze: A system for counteracting heeling forces by standing on the side of a boat wearing a harness with a hook that is attached to a wire attached to the mast.

trim: (1) To pull in a rope or a sail. (2) The set of the sails.

weather mark: Also windward mark. The first turning mark in most races. It is anchored directly upwind of the starting line.

whitecaps: Foamy crests on the top of waves.

winch: A revolving geared drum turned by a handle that provides mechanical advantage and increases the sailor's ability to pull on a rope under load.

windward: Toward the wind, the side the wind blows upon.

Index

About the Authors

Peter Isler is a two-time America's Cup winning navigator, both with Dennis Conner's *Stars & Stripes* team. As a helmsman, tactician, or navigator, he has won a host of major championships around the world, including the Newport–Bermuda Race, Intercollegiate National Dinghy Championship, SORC, Maxi One Design World Championship, and U.S. Olympic Pre-Trials, to name a few. A graduate of Yale University, he was named Intercollegiate Sailor of the Year in 1976. He served as analyst for ESPN's Emmy Award–winning coverage of the 1992 and 1995 America's Cups and is a featured sailing expert on Speedvision and Outdoor Life Networks, as well as the host of the series *Classics* on Speedvision Network. Isler is president of Isler Sailing International, a sports marketing company in San Diego, where he resides with his wife JJ, an Olympic medalist and a four-time sailing World Champion (and coauthor with Peter of the book *Sailing for Dummies*), and their two daughters, Marly and Megan.

Peter Economy is a business writer and the bestselling coauthor of *Managing for Dummies* and *Consulting for Dummies,* as well as many other books and articles on a wide variety of business topics. Consulting editor for *Bob Nelson's Rewarding Employees* newsletter, Economy has more than fifteen years of business management experience. A graduate of Stanford University, he is currently pursuing his MBA at the Edinburgh Business School while cowriting the upcoming books *MBA for Dummies* and *Home-Based Business for Dummies.* He lives in La Jolla, California, with his wife Jan and three children, Peter, Skylar, and Jackson.